WHAT IF?
———————————

YOUR GUIDE TO MAKING THE BEST DECISIONS EVER

EMILJANO CITAKU

© Copyright 2020 - All rights reserved.
Published by Citaku Publishing

It is not legal to reproduce, duplicate, or transmit any part of this document in either electronic means or in printed format. Recording of this publication is strictly prohibited and any storage of this document is not allowed unless with written permission from the publisher except for the use of brief quotations in a book review.

Hardcover: ISBN 978-1-7356823-1-0

Paperback: 978-1-7356823-4-1

Ebook: 978-1-7356823-7-2

www.emiljanocitaku.com

CONTENTS

Introduction	1

PART I
THE UNIVERSE OF CHOICE

1. The Genesis of Choice	9
2. Don't Get Obsessed with Choices	17
3. Go With Your Gut (Trust Yourself)	24
4. Pigeon Superstition	30
5. Bernoulli's Principle	35
6. Why You Make Bad Choices	41
7. Your Choices Influence Others	47
8. The Enigma of the Crystal Ball	54
9. The Differences Between Choices and Decisions	60

PART II
THE UNIVERSE OF DECISION

10. When Your Brain Goes To work	67
11. Avoidance...No Decision Is A Decision	72
12. No Fear!	77
13. Focus, Focus, Focus	83
14. Narrow Down Your Options	87
15. The Devil's Advocate	93
16. Be a Lion Tamer	99
17. Live Without Regrets	105
18. Take a Trip to the Bathroom	110
19. Tame Your Anxiety	116
20. Marshmallows and Instant Gratification	121
21. Alice Learned the Hard Way	127
22. Brew a Better Cup of Tea	133
23. Tools In Your Repertoire	144
Final Words	153
Bibliography	157

INTRODUCTION

MANY OF US FEEL WRACKED BY THE POSSIBLE OUTCOMES OF the road we chose not to travel, or conversely, wracked by the vagaries of the road before us. These feelings always and only lead us to the thorniest of all life's questions: *What if*. *What if* I hadn't married? *What if* I had married a childhood love rather than a collaborator at work? *What if* I hadn't chosen philosophy as my major? *What if* I had accepted that job in New York City? *What if* I bought a home in the suburbs six years ago instead of choosing to rent a condo in town? You suffer the torture of these thoughts as well. We all do.

The *what-ifs* of life exist as ephemeral illusions. It means they don't really exist at all. By choosing one path, all other paths and outcomes immediately cease to exist. Did you ever see *Mr. Nobody*? It began with a central premise that time is fractured into spatial and temporal elements, but time only travels in one direction. One direction cancels out all other options. I know you've probably seen *The Time Traveler's Wife* as well and know that every travel backward in time offers a new reality...but remember, fiction is far from reality. It's not true. One choice precludes all other choices, so *what if* ceases to apply.

The other tangent of thought causes us to suffer through difficult decisions in trying to cover every base and prevent every possible disastrous outcome. Did you ever see *Next*? Nicholas Cage plays a "magician" who can see outcomes a few seconds before they occur. Too bad it's also fiction. You are not a magician. Let me give you a break here: You are mortal, and that's okay.

This book is designed to help you with all those decision-making issues:

- Learn how to make the best possible decision with the least amount of angst.
- Learn how to use intentional choices to your best advantage.
- Learn how to stop regretting your past decisions.
- Learn how to make the issues surrounding even the most complex decisions easier to digest.

As a human being, you have a lot going for you. Your brain stores memory and jumps in with powerful circuitry to help analyze complex options. Your memories hold keys from the past to unlock the future. Your life experience enables you to apply reason in the face of new options. Your mentors offer valuable feedback. I am one of those mentors. My goal is to be with you as you read this book and interact with you as an invisible guest in your deliberations. The moral imperative to walk with the least impact of future generations is a noble precept in dealing with the environment, but the same logic just doesn't transfer across to decision making. Your choice is not one of *will you* impact others, or *how much* you impact others, but whether that impact will be positive or negative.

That may seem arbitrary. but think of the natural properties of our universe. An immutable principle of entropy governs our world, and the same principle governs our lives as well. Briefly stated, it's the order of unpredictability. Random things happen. Good things happen to bad people, and conversely, bad things happen to good people…as the Bible says, *rain falls on the just and the unjust*. Life happens. This leads you to ask, "What did I do to deserve this?" **You may be asking the wrong question. The eternal question is this: Can I change the future, and have an impact on what takes place** *as a result of what has happened*?

Philosophers from the beginning of time offer a resounding chorus of, "Yes!" Aristotle addressed the concept of fatalism as early as 380 B.C. Free will exists, and therefore, fatalism does not exist. Morally, every person on planet earth makes decisions and creates an impact on every other lifeform. Whether you can discern the cause of an event does not mean you cannot have an impact on the final outcome of the event, change it, or eliminate it altogether.

You bear no small responsibility. The *butterfly effect* suggests that a very small action can have a very large impact on a future outcome. Your choices matter. They really do. And rather than letting that suffocate you, I want to help you deal with the whole issue of choice. I want to make it easier for you. I want to help you be known as a (*gasp!*) decisive person.

Like it or not, your boss, your prospective employer, perhaps the person sitting next to you respects the quality of decisiveness. You can see it in adolescent girls who always say, "I'm looking for a confident kind of guy," which is synonymous with tight jeans or a tattoo or some other symbol of brash identity. I want you to stand out as a person who is confident in your ability to make a decision, the right decision, without bravado or looking arrogant. You know the difference, don't you? Who just popped into your head a moment ago? Mmm. You know who I'm talkin' about!

If you have ever felt inadequate, paralyzed between options, and unable to decide, you are *not* an indecisive person. You are a person who lacks decisive skill sets! I want to arm you with the ability to tackle those complicated, thorny decisions like an action hero, earning you respect and filling your mind with self-esteem. Becoming a decision-making wonder just takes the right tools, a paradigm that works, dispelling a few myths, and some practice. That's where I come in! It's my job to bring all this to the table. I have taken all my life experiences, done the hard work of reading the research, and culled all the best thoughts to formulate this instruction. I've put it into bite-sized pieces for easy digestion and am including a recap of important strategies for your use as a workbook in making difficult decisions.

"What If" is your handbook to living a meaningful life with good decision making. My challenge to you is to show up. Be honest. Offer full value. Get to know me. I like famous movie lines. I'm a reader (of course, I'm a writer!). I'm a loyal friend. I never tell secrets, so you can take me to any part of your life without fear of gossip. I sound like a great friend, don't I? I'm also your guide on this quest to living a more meaningful life. Everything I share is something I've tried, and you may feel confident in giving it a whirl. My job is to blaze the way into this new world in which a decision ceases to be your mortal enemy, but a puzzle you can solve without dread or weeks in the sweltering valley of indecision. My promise is to be present when you show up, to be present with the right words for any given situation.

It's your job to read each chapter and respond to what you read. Keep a journal handy to jot down important concepts and things you don't want to forget. Practice making those big decisions with me and learn how easy it is when you ask the right questions and use the right tools.

We make choices in life because life waits for no man or woman. Failure to make a choice *is* a choice and leaves an impact regardless of whether we made an active choice or not. Time is straightforward. You cannot travel backward and change a decision in light of new information. You cannot erase an outcome. You must live your life and make good choices along the way.

Instead of futilely asking *What if...* ask instead, "What if I read this book and become a stellar decision maker? How will my life change?" You're already thinking of some stellar benefits, aren't you? Now ask yourself, conversely, "What if I don't read this book and nothing changes?" Is that an outcome you're ready to accept? Me neither.

I want to live a life of intentional choice. I want to make decisions I can look back upon with a sense of self-fulfillment. Don't you? Let's do this together!

PART I
THE UNIVERSE OF CHOICE

1
THE GENESIS OF CHOICE

"I believe that we are solely responsible for our choices, and we have to accept the consequences of every deed, word, and thought throughout our lifetime."

— Elisabeth Kubler-Ross

Throughout the ages, the concept of choice versus fate (or predestination) has roiled but never been proven. Tomes of philosophy litter library shelves, and in the end, each decides on his/her own belief system. Sure, Kant may have some excellent theories on fatalism, but in the end, it's your own personal beliefs that determine how you make personal choices.

That said, you may feel a little foggy on these schools of thought, or perhaps never been exposed to a thorough course on philosophy, so let's cover the definition of each. The genesis of choice has *everything* to do with the way you make choices, so this underlying premise cannot be ignored.

What is your philosophy of life? Proponents of free agency believe everyone acts and is free to act outside the realm of universal law. Of course, we all believe in gravity, but you have the choice of defying gravity, in donning wings and jumping off a cliff. It may end disastrously, but you have that choice. You are a free agent, like any sports celebrity seeking to be chosen for a team.

Kant and other fatalists would suggest your future is inevitable. Destiny has been written, and you are acting out your fate every day. The supposed choices you make are precluded by circumstances beyond your control. As much as you might want to fly in the face of societal constraints, you are bound by them. It is out of your hands.

Proponents of predestination differ from fatalists in that your life's story has been written by a power other than your own. That power controls fate. It engineers your decisions. Like Truman in *The Truman Show*, you are being manipulated into a story over which no one, not yourself nor those around you, offer one iota of control.

Now in reading this, you're already aware that each theory holds a kernel of truth. In some choices, you are a free agent. In other choices, society may preclude your options. In other situations, you may feel the stars have aligned, and your choice has been made for you. In other words, your belief system may not be arbitrary and may yet be true. That's okay. You are more complex than a small paragraph of a simplified description.

The important thing is actually to think about these esoteric questions of life. What you believe will influence your choices, your morals, and the important life decisions you make. Few of us sit down on a Sunday afternoon and write out our philosophy of life. We don't need to...but we do need to be aware, or else life's choices become incongruent, and problems arise.

For example, if you believe in loyalty within a relationship but also believe that an irresistible desire for someone outside the relationship is in the stars, your next choice produces a moral paradox. The potential for hurting yourself or another, along with your reputation in living a life congruent with your values, stands in the troubled waters of choice. Integrity comes from knowing your values and being willing to live by them, even when no one else is looking. **It begins with knowing your own values.**

One's code of ethics is sometimes part and parcel of a religious or social life, and sometimes a set of personal rules, but *always* the basis of choice. Sociopaths careen through life only doing what pleases or benefits themselves, and they ping off everyone around them, leaving a storm of harm or confusion in their wake. Psychopaths put aside all societal norms, never able to grasp the concepts of right or wrong.

Civilization is based on the majority of citizens accepting a code of ethics with enough commonalities to ensure they are able to peacefully rub shoulders and benefit one another. A sudden influx of pathology or a clash with the addition of a foreign value system creates an unavoidable problem. That's why ethnic cultures immigrating to another country find pockets of those with their own background for neighbors. That's why the emergence of a psychopathic serial killer puts a community into panic. That deviance from the norm engenders fear and danger.

So let's get down to brass tacks. What is your value system? Do you share it with others in your circle? Is the basis of your choice and complex decision-making?

- Begin to write down your philosophy of life. Are you an agent of free choice, a fatalist, or has everything been predetermined by another power? Of course, you're a mix of all three, but figure it out. Write it down.
- List some of your recent choices. How was each choice reached?
- Find a good title of the philosophy you find yourself leaning toward. Read up on it. Distill what you read into chapter summaries and be sure you know yourself inside and out.
- Whom do you know who differs from you? Do you get along well? Does your conflicting basis of decision-making ever clash?

Once you feel like you have a handle on your belief system, you're ready to start analyzing the choices you make. In most instances, you make choices based on relative assignments of positive and negative consequences. If a choice is determined to be mostly positive, you swallow the negatives and proceed. If the negatives outweigh the positives, you choose to ignore the option. Realize that those positives and negatives are intangible, and their relative weight is determined subjectively. That's okay. That's life. Just be aware that how you define what is positive and how you weight it may not be the same as someone within your circle. Offer respect as you wish to receive it.

The paradox of choice. The paradox of choice surfaced in the course of psychological study with the interesting hypothesis that too many options actually decreases odds of an end result happening, of making any choice at all. One memorable study offered shoppers six jams to choose from and tracked their purchases. Another set of shoppers were offered an array of twenty-five choices. Do you want to guess which set bought more jam? The shoppers with fewer choices found it easier to make a choice and went home with more marmalade for their toast.

The paradox of choice proves that, in some instances, more is not more. Less is more. How do we make that relative to your own complicated life? For one thing, shy away from choices with too many options, especially if you know that you will labor and stew over each choice you make. Further, resist the temptation to offer too many choices to others. Your child cannot make a decision even you would have trouble making. If your friend has trouble making decisions and it drives you bonkers, limit the options you offer. Yes, it is that easy.

The axiom of choice. Mathematicians have proven a theory (of course they have), which says (simply put) that in every set of options, there is an intuitive choice presented. As arbitrary as it sounds, and as impossible as it might be in the universe of all decisions, it nevertheless can make many of our choices a lot easier. Let's look at an easy example. In any bin of shoes, it should be possible to find a set. That's the crucible of choice. When we take that principle and apply it to choosing one of Baskin & Robbin's 32 flavors of ice cream, that crucible explodes.

Does that mean the theory is a bunch of hogwash? No, just that it has its limits. In any choice, it is easier if we begin by looking for an easy pick out of all the options. We see ample evidence of this in the natural world around us. A fox hunts for game. It can sniff along the river bank where all animals have to come for a drink of water, or it can sniff out little rabbits in their likely hiding places. A simple choice. It makes one, and does it look tortured in the process? No, it actually looks rather happy with the decision. If it doesn't find a bunny on the riverbank, it moves to the forest. Does it look like it's beating itself up for looking at the riverbank? No, it just moves on.

The axiom of choice can be very simple upon occasion. Make a simple choice. Evaluate it. Stay or choose again, depending on the outcome. Be brave enough to just move on.

Evaluate along the way. Many of life's most important decisions fall outside all theoretical realms. Should you have a savings plan? Should you marry this person? Should you have a family? Should you buy this property? So many of life's big decisions begin with little choices. You start a job, and if you mark a box to divert some earnings into savings, the potential for having a usable bankroll five years from now is a huge impact. Was it part of some large decision?

You choose to go to a particular party one night and choose to visit with someone. Sharing a love of Star Wars leads to a meeting for coffee. Three months down the road, you may be considering marriage...a huge decision based on a small random choice. An old Disney flick presented this concept well. In *Never Cry Wolf,* a researcher ends up spending a winter in the frozen tundra to examine the species *canine lupus*. In the long train ride west, the lead character begins to question, "How did I end up here? Was this a mistake of jumbled papers? Did I really volunteer?" He ends up realizing the futility of survival if it all rests on his own experience. You'll have to watch the movie for yourself to find out what happens...the point is what interests us here: sometimes the simplest of choices leads to the biggest of outcomes.

The best way to make a choice you won't regret is to live like you are part of the checkerboard of life. You know how you sometimes make a move, holding onto that checker to be sure it isn't a mistake? In life, we call it being *circumspect*. Think about leaving the house for an errand. We look around us, feel our clothes, make sure our keys are stowed away, and think, "Ah, yes. All is well." Now take that a step further. You meet someone at a party. You have a lot in common, so you agree to meet up over coffee. Does it feel right? Go. You meet at coffee and agree to go out for dinner. Does it feel right? Go. See what I mean? You evaluate each step as you take it, and the result is never second-guessing yourself. *What if I hadn't gone to the party? What if I had sat on the other side of the room?* These questions are irrelevant. What matters is how you approach the simple *next question*. Many of life's disastrous choices can be averted with careful attention to each step along the decision-making pathway.

Ultimately, we each strive to be happy and feel self-fulfilled. Those are often seen as results, but what if happiness is a choice? What if you get to choose every day to see the bright side, to enjoy optimism, to cultivate hope, to *feel* happy? The crux of your existence is like the teeter-totter, and the beginning of all choice is the initial decision to live life intentionally. Choose to be happy. Choose to make good choices. That can be hard, so you have me at your side to help you along the way.

Chapter Summary

Nothing you do, say or choose, exists in a vacuum. You are a part of your own philosophy of life. You are part of the norms of the tribe you call your own. A congruent life implies thought and relevance in choosing the big (and little) things in life.

- You get to formulate your own philosophy of life. Be intentional in what you believe.
- Understand how you have made choices in the past. Has it served you well? If not, employ some better strategies.
- Think about the effects of each small choice leading up to a big choice. Pay attention to danger signals, as well as confirmations you are on the right path.

In the next chapter, you will learn what happens when you obsess over a choice and how to avoid falling into that trap.

2
DON'T GET OBSESSED WITH CHOICES

"In a world where we have too many choices and too little time, the obvious thing to do is just ignore stuff."

— SETH GODIN

HAVE YOU EVER SEEN A CHILD PARALYZED BY CHOICE? WHICH cookie... the chocolate chip or the iced cookie with sprinkles? You can feel the palpable angst because you are no stranger to this sensation, yourself. We all remember, and possibly recently, getting paralyzed by choices and feeling powerless to choose between two (or more) unknown outcomes. In a world where choices abound, this becomes even more problematic.

Our grandparents lived in a simpler society. A trip to the general store to buy shoes only offered a choice between serviceable wear and fancy wear. Boom! Done. The choice is made. The Industrial Age may not have done us any favors. Now a trip to buy shoes involves a plethora of manufacturers, styles, and claimed values, and the angst of that choice is painful. Sometimes we simply don't know if we'll feel comfortable in the shoe after a week of walking in it. Sometimes we don't know if the color will stay vibrant, if the white will stay white, and if the heel will meet our needs. Then we look at the styles available, and whoa! The choice of a new pair of shoes just got way too complicated. Have you ever wanted to set out three options and call out, "Attention Walmart shoppers! Choose my next pair of shoes." Life would be much easier if we didn't have to make that choice.

Shoes represent just one of the hundreds of choices we make each day. Should we carry a wrap? Will it be bothersome? Will we get cold if we don't have it? Yikes, it's no wonder 21st-century adults get obsessed with choices. We expect ourselves to be able to handle it all, but clearly, our world of choice is out of control. The simple truth is that the more choices we have, the less satisfied we may be with the outcome. The plethora of *too much* hinders us in making the best choice possible.

Don't despair. What you are feeling is normal, and it's a defining problem for this generation. Young adults today are struggling with choices over everything from an ideal bedtime to the allocation of resources. Let's separate issues of impulse control from complex decision-making, which we will cover in-depth in Part II. Let's focus for a moment on choices affected by self-discipline.

Correcting self-indulgence in choice obsession. Some choice obsession falls into this category of choosing what we know is good for us as opposed to choosing what we *want or think we want*. Learning how to limit self-indulgence removes some of the angst from these forms of choices. Let's look at two examples. Should you turn out the light or indulge in just one more (chapter, episode)....you fill in the blank. You know your own temptations. You know how much sleep you need, how well you function with less sleep, and you have an idea what tomorrow's responsibilities look like. Why is this such a difficult choice? Is there anything wrong with the activities we enjoy? Probably not.

It's hard because many of us have failed to learn or apply self-discipline to our lives. Many are raised in permissive homes, where discipline was never translated into habits of self-discipline. Some of us think the rules don't really apply to us. We got a free pass once too often, and the result is a flagrant disregard of reality. And some of us are just plain self-indulgent. Products of a hedonistic society, we're like the grasshopper in Aesop's fable, and really just want to have a good time all the time.

Correcting this requires us to knuckle down to some inner rules. Set a bedtime. Go to bed. Self-discipline is a gift you can give yourself that just keeps on giving. Get enough sleep, live a healthier life. Live a healthier life, spend less on medicine, more on fun. The value of self-discipline cannot be disputed.

Another example in which a lack of self-discipline hinders us in making choices is in the spending of money. We get used to having things. Sometimes buying on credit is too easy. We fail to implement any form of self-denial when it comes to putting off an expenditure. In this scenario, we *know* we shouldn't indulge, but *we have trouble resisting the temptation to buy it.* Let's remove the factors, again, of complex decisions. We aren't talking about buying a new car here. We're talking about frittering away our money on something we know we probably shouldn't purchase, but we get caught mentally shifting from one foot to another on hot stones because *we just really want it.* Is there anything wrong with things we buy on a whim? Not in and of themselves, but without self-discipline, these choices paralyze us and can harm us down the road.

Correcting this requires us to knuckle down to some inner rules. Set a budget. Live within your means. Failure to do so leads to some pretty obvious fails, doesn't it?

From frittering time to putting off folding the laundry, these itty bitty daily choices can become stumbling blocks. One day that self-indulgence suddenly bites us with an overdrawn account or a living room overflowing with laundry baskets as someone knocks on the door. Our obsession with so many choices and how to make an intelligent choice has become a stumbling block.

Choosing the better of two goods. This area of choice obsession troubles the best of us. It begins with decreasing the confusion of too many options: narrow the field down from six kinds of cake to our two favorites, the chocolate cake or the carrot cake. We like them both. Great options. Neither is better or worse than the other because really, those carrots in the cake are not really a serving of vegetables, are they? Sugar is sugar. Again, let's remove the complex decisions from our everyday stumbling blocks. Which piece of cake will you choose?

Two goods are problematic because you shouldn't have them both. In terms of cost, health, and space, you don't need and shouldn't have everything you like. From cake to gadgets, how do you draw the line? How do you make these choices? This delightful dilemma can be painful and a lot less than delightful if you don't learn how to make effective choices. Ask yourself some quick questions:

- Can I afford this?
- Can I return this?
- Do I need this?

- Do I have a place to put this?
- Does one set of preferences outweigh the other?
- Will I value this a month from now?
- Do I have anything similar at home already?

These questions make a difference for all those spontaneous choices you make each day. *A choice needs to garner at least three yeses to make it into the acceptable side of the equation.* You may be able to afford it, and you may be able to return it, but if you don't need it or have a place for it and can't promise to use it a month from now, it's a no-go. See how that works? You must decide between two evening entertainments. Can you afford one over the other? Does one set of preferences outweigh the other? Will you enjoy the memory a month from now? Earn three yeses, or it's a no-go.

Choices become easier to make with practice. Apply a paradigm for making a choice on a consistent basis, and you'll be surprised how easy it becomes a month from now.

Don't let time hold you hostage. One of the most common forms of choice obsession relates to how much time a good choice takes. All too often, it ends up taking us far too long. Time is relative, so let's abandon the absolutes of how many minutes it should take you to choose a greeting card. Instead, look honestly at your own schedule. Where do you feel like you are hampered by the time it takes to make a choice? There are ways to liberate yourself from time paralysis.

- Start keeping track of how long it actually takes to make a choice. You may find that you're choosing faster than you thought, or it may confirm too much precious time has been

allocated on something the universe finds mundane. Collect data.
- Group your shots. Going back to the example of choosing a greeting card - why not choose cards for the next six birthdays at the same time? The odds that each card you pick up will be suitable for someone on your list shortens the time overall.
- Don't look back. You've made a choice, Move on.
- Stop comparing apples to oranges. The unknowns between choices become ticking bombs when you get obsessed with how one compares to another. We are rarely trying to decide between a blue pen or a green pen. Most of our choices are multifaceted and defy comparison.
- Set a time limit. If you routinely obsess over choosing a greeting card, set the alarm on your watch and limit how much time you spend on choosing the next card you purchase. This limit setting will improve your ability to make good choices if you continue the practice.

Choice obsession is rarely pathological. Most of us who suffer choice obsession end up making choices. Those choices do not become lifelong obsessions, but the tendency to make choosing a pair of shoes as important as choosing your next car is a common form of choice paralysis. Each small decision assumes an inordinate amount of time and energy if we let it do so, and you are the person holding the reins. You get to decide if taking thirty minutes to choose a greeting card is excessive or if a five-minute perusal of the racks is too casual an effort for the relationship at stake.

These judgment calls form the basis of your satisfaction of life, and ultimately, your sense of comfort in your own skin. Read and read this chapter again, making notes of your thoughts in a journal. The process of self-examination is required to assess if you are obsessed with choices, and your response affects not just how you see yourself but also how others view you.

Chapter Summary

Choice paralysis leads to the tendency to obsess over all your choices. This is counterproductive to your lifestyle and how you want others to perceive you. Learning how to make efficient choices is a skill well worth learning.

- Limit self-indulgence to special occasions, and you will find it easier to make choices.
- In a choice between two goods, realize that either choice works. Apply a paradigm to make this faster and easier.
- Time either works for you or against you when it comes to making choices. Only you can decide if you're obsessing or being realistic. Make time your friend.

In the next chapter, you will learn how to trust your basic instincts.

3

GO WITH YOUR GUT (TRUST YOURSELF)

"Trust your instinct to the end, though you can render no reason."

— Ralph Waldo Emerson

NCIS is an award-winning television show in which the lead investigator always goes with his gut. What does that even mean? Gibbs solves every case using his famous gut, and for a long time, this was a mystery to me. I had to do some digging. Let me share what I discovered.

There is nothing mystical about gut instinct. Below the level of cognitive reasoning lies a wealth of personal knowledge. It is based on the interlacing of many experiences to form a subconscious realization without fact or reasoning. It's something children understand before we train them to ignore what they sense in favor of what they think.

One of the best examples is from the Disney movie *Bambi*. The hungry deer go to the plain in search of food. When pausing at the edge of the forest, Bambi's mother knows it is dangerous. She sniffs the air. She listens. She looks long and hard at the open expanse. The music offers additional impact, and we're all silently whispering, "Don't go in there. Don't go in there." She disregards her instinct and goes anyway, and of course, she pays for that lapse in judgment with her life.

Children delve deep into their instinctive reserves to form judgments, and they do so without any sense of embarrassment. They like someone, or they don't. They trust an adult, or they don't. There is no explanation. There is no apology. It just is what it is. They trust those instincts implicitly.

Do you remember the first time someone tried to dissuade you from your instinctive knowledge of something? For most girls, it comes with the admonition to *be nice*. Ignore the sense of danger, be polite. For boys, it is often attached to the pressure to be courageous. But it begins much earlier. As a matter of fact, we begin teaching children to ignore their instincts from the git-go. *Give Auntie a kiss. Respect all adults. Be polite.* Slowly but surely, as we teach them the rudiments of civility, we also teach them to abandon their inner knowing. Should we? Can it be reclaimed?

Psychologists studying adults now know that these instincts are the result of swift cognitive readings from years of experience. Your brain is a fantastic reservoir of information, both what you sense on the surface of things as well as all that resides below your level of consciousness. Let's think of an example we can all understand. You are walking through a parking lot, and a car slows down. The driver rolls down a window to ask you a question, and a sudden sense of apprehension sweeps over you.

In the space of a few seconds, your brain processes thousands of impressions. The car. Its appearance. The mud on the door. The man with a hat obscuring his face. Your isolation. A rough voice...and the list goes on. From everything you've experienced comes a signal of alarm. Pay attention to that alarm. Now is not the time to be nice. Now is the time to save yourself. Your gut has just intervened to save your life.

You may have felt butterflies in your stomach, your mouth may have been dry, and you may have felt slightly faint, but let's be realistic. It didn't come from your intestines. It came from the myriad of neural connections in your brain, which are interlaced and lighting up faster than a hotel switchboard. Your brain acts without your permission with every breath you take, with the way you instinctively put out an arm to steady yourself, and with each beat of your heart. That's the autonomic nervous system. It is part of your fight or flight mechanism for self-preservation.

Those connections extend into the reasoning, thinking, and remembering parts of your brain as well, assimilating information and prompting a response in the blink of an eye. That's your gut instinct, and if you've been overruling your innate knowledge of things, it's time to resurrect that primeval trust in yourself. Easier said than done, though, right?

- Begin by acknowledging your inner knowing. When a thought surfaces, say it to yourself. If you can, say it out loud. If not, just consciously think it in your mind. Begin to write down these little "knowing" incidents. You will begin to see a pattern, learn to recognize a hunch, and develop confidence in following those hunches.
- Continue building confidence in your instincts by simply going with them, pedal to the metal. Recognize that successful choices are

accompanied by effort, and focused effort at that. When you go with a gut reaction, give it all you've got, and if it proves successful, your justification for trusting your instincts intensifies. You sabotage your instincts with a half-hearted commitment to a course of action. When an effort doesn't pan out, you assume it is because your instinctive choice was wrong, when that may not have been the case at all.

- Be flexible in your idea of how it is supposed to happen. All too often, we lock ourselves into a mental picture of what the results of a choice should look like and how to make choices happen. Reality seldom follows our personal rules for the universe. I know, right? We envision a reality that never transpires, and in the process, we lose faith in our instincts. Being open to yourself requires an openness to the universe at large.
- Begin a journal detailing your instinctive choices. Write down how that sense of knowing what to do came to you, how it played out, and the final result. This becomes the matrix of your belief in yourself, and over time, your confidence will grow. The adage is true: *We live our lives forward, but understanding comes from looking backward.* Understanding never grows within a vacuum. You must cultivate that inner wisdom, and the easiest way is by associating your past with your present.
- Read books about choice. An excellent title is *Women Who Run With the Wolves* by Clarissa Pinkola Estes. Her Ph.D. in psychology, along

> with her family background, formed the basis for her translation of myth into knowing. She recognized that many of us are instinct-deprived because of our dependence on a fact-based upbringing, and suggests we go back to the basics to learn self-trust of our instincts. Don't get hung up on the feminine slant, because much of her writing applies to all human beings regardless of gender.

It doesn't matter where you fall on the continuum of trusting your instincts or applying reasoning to every decision. Recognize that our life-knowledge is like an iceberg. Much of what we see reflects only a small portion of the reality under the surface. Don't automatically debunk the world of instincts; rather, expand your awareness and learn new truths.

Did you ever read *Blink?* It's not a new book, but the concept is still talked about today. The author suggested those snap decisions, just relying on gut instincts, are the basis of many *good* decisions. Science has borne him out on that premise. Your gut is a powerful ally in making a *good* snap decision. It isn't based on whim, but rather on the pattern of past experience for which you have an emotional reaction. Thus it feels like emotion. It fails to register on the barometer of conscious thought, but it doesn't pop up out of nowhere. Learn to trust it once in a while!

Split-second choices always result from this inner knowing, so ignore them at your own peril. Not every decision is awarded the time, reflection, and study to make it a "good" decision. Your choice of whether to walk through a dark parking lot may seem more like walking through a minefield, and no amount of *knowledge* will prepare you for the necessity of recognizing danger and responding appropriately. This inner knowing does not supplant reasoned decision making. Inner knowing exists on a parallel level of cognizance. Learn to trust your choices made on instinct.

Chapter Summary

Gut instincts deserve their place in the decision-making zone of self-awareness. Many of the instantaneous choices you make are derived almost solely from your prior experience and inner knowing. Strengthen that sense of self.

- Inculcate your own life rules as you get in touch with basic instincts.
- Learn to recognize instinctive warnings *and trust them!*
- Apply yourself to understanding how your instincts work, and do it intentionally. Your choices will improve, and you will develop confidence in your instincts.

In the next chapter, you will learn how we fool ourselves into making choices on false premises, and how to avoid that pitfall.

4

PIGEON SUPERSTITION

*"The root of all superstition is that men observe
when a thing hits,
but not when it misses."*

— Francis Bacon

About now, you may be wondering, "What???" I want to introduce you to a fabulous study conducted by the renowned pioneer in cognitive reasoning, B.F. Skinner. More than that, I want you to understand how that relates to the choices you make and how to make better choices.

Skinner conducted a foundational study on pigeons. He began by putting these caged birds on a diet, so they would feel perpetually hungry. Seems a little unkind, doesn't it? Skinner then devised a way of releasing pellets of food at predetermined times, and of course, hungry pigeons were interested, always looking for the next morsel of food. He then sat back and watched their behavior, taking notes.

What he discovered shed a lot of light on how we make choices based on past experience, and the implications proved enormous. The pigeons did random pigeon things, and each bird responded to the dropped pellet of food based on its prior action. For example, one bird had turned around in its cage three times when the pellet dropped. It applied that same action and discovered, quite erroneously, that it worked! If it kept turning around three times, the pellets kept coming. That poor bird brain put two and two together and came up with the wrong answer. You already know the pellet dropped despite the bird's behavior, but the pigeon didn't know this. It developed a superstition concerning how to get its food.

Another pigeon noticed that a pellet dropped when it bobbed its head. Thus began intense head bobbing, signaling, "More food, please." Nothing changed the poor bird's mind once the superstition began. If it bobbed three separate times before the pellet dropped, then maybe the gods of the pellet world didn't see it, maybe the head bobbing wasn't pronounced enough...the poor pigeon kept bobbing for food,

The interesting conclusion was that each bird developed its own superstition about the source of pellets based upon its own experience. The random conclusions proved unique to the bird in each cage. Now you're probably wondering, "What on earth does this have to do with me?"

This became the beginning of behavioral psychology, and in the years since Skinner's foundational work, it has become its own genre of psychological study. The field of behavioral psychology looks at why you and I act the way we do, and these proponents have concluded that we might not be any smarter than pigeons. Before you get offended, think about the ways you have seen it manifested in others.

Did you ever see *A League of Their Own?* A group of ladies started a baseball league in World War II while the men were at war, and each had her own winning superstition. One wore the same stinky socks to every game. Ewww! Manager Tom Hanks says, "You're killing me!" and I can imagine what the locker room smelled like, can't you? Many professional players still do that today.

These superstitions are manifestations of the same pigeon reasoning Skinner studied years ago. Win a game, try to mimic the same behaviors, and superstition is born. It hovers over every aspect of life, not just sports.

One recent article in Inc. listed twenty ways to attract *good luck*. We want to exercise some control over the fickle outcomes of nature, so we engineer behaviors or philosophies to guarantee the outcomes. One revolved around the ancient principle of casting your bread upon the water. *Do more good, and more good will come your way.* It's like refining the principle of karma and forcing it into certain behavioral outcomes. Is there anything wrong with doing more good? Of course not. As human beings, fostering good is part of our civilization. Will doing good bring more good? Often it will, but what happens when doing good becomes predicated on the outcomes, and the outcomes fail to pan out?

Disappointed do-gooders may stop doing good because it just doesn't pay off. Hence the phrase, "No good deed goes unpunished." A new superstition is born. Some may develop a greedy outlook, no longer doing good for the sake of benefiting others, but only to benefit themselves. How sad for our society. Others may do good to only some and in some situations, making personal judgments about the most deserving or worthwhile recipients. Again, the outcomes become skewed.

Skinner initiated Behavioral Psychology back in the 1940s. Do his studies remain true today? Scientists replicating Skinner's work have had the advantage of technological innovations. They recorded sound and auditory signals of pigeons, much like you or I might see or hear and verified that, yes, pigeons (and by extrapolation, people) are prone to reducing choices to intricate behaviors leading to superstition. The addition of sound and auditory signals proved what many knew all along, a repeated phrase or motto is also a part of pigeon superstition. Yes, we may be more like pigeons than we once thought. Look at your own life and find the parallels. Think of one behavior which you perform because it's lucky, be it carrying a talisman, wearing a certain article of clothing, or uttering a certain phrase. The odds are, you can think of at least one "lucky" behavior or trait. The fact that despite our ability to reason and determine whether or not an expected outcome *always occurs to* reinforce our behavior, we continue anyway and the failure ceases to cause us any dissonance. We want to believe it is true, so we continue to *make* it true.

We come now full circle to wanting to influence the fates, guarantee outcomes, and are willing to infer whatever we want in the process. The mythology becomes inculcated into family lore, and we try to perpetuate these processes with never a thought as to how illogical our behaviors may be. It's part of the alchemy of family and family mores, passed down from one generation to another. I love it. I just want you to be aware that sometimes your choices are not predicated on thoughtful or factual conclusions. They are based on the superstition of pigeons, God help us!

These superstitions work for us in eliminating the angst of many choices we make throughout life, but just how valuable is pigeon superstition when it comes to deciding which of two jobs to take, whether or not to marry a certain person, or which house to purchase? The more heavily weighted the decision we need to make, the less the choice of superstition serves us. But in deciding what to wear to that first interview, or which table to occupy in a restaurant...I'm comfortable with pigeon superstition if you are!

Chapter Summary

Everyone tries to ward off fate and control destiny by using superstitions in making choices. It may sound crazy, but it's true. The important thing is to take a good hard look at yourself and figure out your own superstitions. Then decide if you want to base major life decisions based on them. Consciously decide how you will make major choices in life.

- Make a list of some of your own superstitions, and be honest. We are all riddled with foibles.
- Decide what kind of choices you are comfortable relegating to the superstition of pigeons.
- Decide which major life decisions need to be made in a different way. We'll get to that in Part II.

In the next chapter, you will learn how often you play the odds in making decisions and determine how well that is working for you.

5

BERNOULLI'S PRINCIPLE

> *"If children have the ability to ignore all odds and percentages, then maybe we can learn from them. When you think about it, what other choice is there but to hope? We have two options, medically and emotionally: give up, or Fight Like Hell."*
>
> — Lance Armstrong

Are you a science buff? I wasn't a stellar student while I was growing up, so when I first heard this principle applied to the idea of how our choices are made, I was intrigued. I seemed to remember it being something about air pressure, and I thought, "What? This has got to be *wayyyy* out there. I was wrong. Again.

First of all, let's ignore the math. We're not calculating fluid dynamics, and this isn't a physics class. So what does this obscure principle have to do with the little pathways in your brain? Let's go back to the basic concept. I'm going to speak simply, because I am a simple person. I like to get down to the nitty-gritty. Think of a fluid flowing through a horizontal pipe. Daniel Bernoulli calculated a formula for figuring out how the pressure of a constricted part influenced the flow of the whole. I finally remembered something about that from a long-ago physics class, and my response was still, "So what?"

Take it a step further and integrate it with the fabulous thing we call the mind. We can take a simplistic version of the concept and reduce it to something that makes sense:

Odds of Gain X + Value of Gain = Expected Value

What are the odds of gain in any given situation? Suppose you are asked to pick up an odd job, and you are offered an hourly wage. The odds of it being a four-hour job are worth more than if it's a two-hour job. If it's an eight-hour job, does it suddenly become less appealing? These human variables are not quantifiable anywhere apart from inside your head and according to your own value system. But let's assume you are offered a four-hour gig at an hourly rate. Odds are, you will earn a sum you can use in a special project.

What is the value of the gain? Suppose my project is buying a new car. Will that four-hour gig prove all that helpful? Perhaps not. What if, instead, I am planning a weekend getaway? How about now? The value is intrinsic within your own value system. No one can assign value but you. But let's assume you're wanting a getaway, and you are really looking forward to this trip, so it's of great value to you.

Okay, we apply the odds to the value to figure out the EXPECTED value. See what a difference emphasizing a single word makes? What you walk away with at the end of the four-hour gig is going to be what it is, and you won't have a lot of power to affect that amount. What it costs to get away is what it costs. You probably won't be negotiating the cost of meals and hotels and transportation. So the expected value relates to how far you *hope it will stretch* toward your goal.

In making choices, we subconsciously employ this reasoning over and over again. We seldom formalize the process, and often we aren't even aware of making these assessments, but believe me, we are. All the time.

Making conscious choices is hard because so much of it rests on the obscure. You have no way of knowing if things will work out the way you want, so you take it on faith, but oddsmakers are a different story. In the world of making bets, this is important stuff. Statistical calculations go into establishing odds, and professional gamblers know just how to determine the best bet in any game of chance.

What do they know that we don't? Again, let's keep it simple. They know that the odds of something happening exactly the same way are affected by the number of chances. So let's suppose you are flicking a spinner on a game board. What are the odds that it will fall in the same place again? If there are five pieces in the pie as it whirls around, the odds when there are five people playing the game are $\frac{1}{5}$ times one, $\frac{1}{5}$ times 2, $\frac{1}{5}$ times 3, $\frac{1}{5}$ times 4 and $\frac{1}{5}$ times 5, with all the values added together. It's a one in five chance for the second try, but with each successive trial, the probability of the spinner landing in the same place increases.

Do you see where I'm going here? In the small repetitious choices, odds add up in your favor. In the biggest life and death decisions where there is no perfect solution, you may also calculate the risks and take a leap of faith...but the risk is much higher.

Do you see the problem inherent in assigning life's most

important decisions to a matter of playing the odds? First of all, it's not uncommon to underestimate the odds. How often have you or a friend looked at a risky decision and thought, "What are the odds? Let's go for it!" Be honest. These are almost always bad choices because your assessment of the odds are made off the fly and are seldom accurate. If the odds shrink by 50% in the course of surviving a jump into a lake from 50 feet, you can see the disastrous outcome, right?

A second reason why this theory proves disastrous is in your anticipation of the expected value. For example, you decide to purchase a new computer. You go and look at several, and you see one in the store that is lightning quick, and you fall in love with it. Your expected value is high, right? When you get it home you are reminded of the bleak reality...speed depends on how it is configured, what is put into the hard drive, how easy it is to find the file you're looking for and a host of other techie questions that the salesperson isn't there to answer. Suddenly you experience buyer's remorse. It isn't the experience you hoped for after all. Your perception of the value you would receive doesn't match the reality of the value you hold in hand. Oops!

Life's little choices are fun to make on the spur of the moment. Bear in mind the word *little*. Deciding on how to spend $10 for afternoon entertainment is not the same as spending $20,000 on a new car. Deciding who to take to the party is not the same as deciding who to marry. One class of choices can be made on playing the odds. The enormity of other decisions preclude a glib choice, don't they?

But all too often, we see people who fail to prioritize the difference between a spur of the moment choice and a major life decision. My goal is to help you reframe your choices into those correct parameters leading to happiness, not regret.

What can you do to improve the result?

- Ask questions. Lots of them. Discerning questions over the value, experience, cost, repairs, etc. all provide you a more realistic framework for realistic expectations. Ask about observed outcomes. How many people do you know who have bought this same product and been happy with it? What does your company do to stand behind the product, thereby increasing the odds of satisfaction? Is the product reviewed in any literature?

These questions are designed to build in a time factor that many snap decisions lack. By asking questions, you have time to *think* about the odds, the cost, and the expected value. Those moments are crucial. Yes, time is your friend. Making a good decision based on the odds always offers a better outcome if the input of information is improved.

- Focus on the possible outcomes. Take time to imagine both the positive and negative possible outcomes. What will a negative outcome cost you? Who else has made this same choice? What was the outcome then? Did you notice something in the first action that appeared in the second action? It was time.

Time is your weapon in producing a happy outcome to any decision based on the odds of perceived value. Time changes the alchemy of making a good choice based on odds and adds a safety net most snap decisions lack. Will you sometimes experience disappointment? Yes, not every outcome will go as expected. But will you reduce the number of disasters? Yes, you will. If you are a fan of playing the odds and like to make decisions by the seat of your pants, add a timeout into the equation. Stop and think to enjoy better outcomes.

Chapter Summary

Sometimes you'll make choices based on the odds of what gains are worth and must assess that risk against the perceived value of what it will be worth to you. Choices based on Bernoulli's Principle offer a rush of adrenaline, but is it worth it?

- Be sure what you expect to enjoy is congruent with reality.
- Reduce the risk of unhappiness by asking questions.
- Spend some time weighing the different factors involved in the decision.
- Utilize this strategy for choices other than life-changing decisions.

In the next chapter, you will focus on why you sometimes made really bad choices, and what you can do about that.

6

WHY YOU MAKE BAD CHOICES

"Bad choices make good stories."

— Margaret Trudeau

How many times have you looked at a friend or loved one and thought, "Why on earth did...?" And if you're honest, you've looked back at some of your own decisions with a humble mind's eye. I know I have, and it's part of the human condition. We all fall victim to bad choices upon occasion.

A wounded, cornered animal bites the helping hand. First and foremost, like any trapped or hurt animal, we all fall victim to bad decisions when we suffer trauma. Universally, the cognitive mind shuts down during trauma, and we tend to function on autopilot. This is never the time to make a major life decision. Choosing from the Starbucks menu is hard enough! Soliciting the help of a friend or helper may feel threatening, and you may want to be alone. This is you determining what is best for you.

Realize as well that past traumas can leave you permanently wounded, impeding your ability to make good choices going forward. If a hurtful background impacts your current choices, you need to take intentional, decisive action to make a change. I'm not suggesting a round of expensive professional therapy, but a time of introspection and personal closing of open wounds.

- Start a journal. You've read this suggestion before, but for this situation, you need to take an internal journey through wilderness areas. The journal becomes your roadmap. Your response to past events represents the switchbacks, and your growing self-awareness is the elevation to greater vistas of illumination. Write. Journaling serves as a catharsis for handling difficult emotions. It is also a way of personal realization. Just do it. Write.
- Find a good book to read. It may be a work of fiction like Jane Eyre, in which the protagonist journeys through a painful childhood to a life of integrity and productivity. It may be a memoir of someone whose life you find relevant to your own. It may be the essays of a psychologist. The title and content of the book are less important than the wealth of experience you find thought-provoking.
- Nurture yourself. I'm not talking about bingeing on chocolate, but about intentional self-care. Be aware of your own needs, and take the time to fix yourself. Ultimately each of us is responsible for ourselves and only ourselves. It doesn't matter who caused your pain and if the person is sorry. You are responsible for you.

Break the cycle. We all know someone who keeps making the same bad choices over and over again. A classic example might be a woman who marries an abusive drunk, divorces, and then marries a workaholic. These two spouses sound very different, but each is addicted to something other than a healthy marital relationship. Failure to break a cycle perpetuates the cycle.

The habit of perpetuating mistakes is often seen in families. A parent is abusive. The child may grow up despising the abusive parent but, fixated on the parent, ends up causing just as much harm to their own child because the cycle was never broken. Another example may be in order. Perhaps, again, a child grows up with an alcoholic parent. The child vows never to marry a drunk and never be a drunk. That sounds reasonable. But in growing up, the emotional lack is often perpetuated in other destructive behaviors. This new grown-up may be emotionally unavailable, demanding, or absent much of the time. It's great they're not a drunk. It's not great that the cycle remained unbroken.

We make bad choices when we are a product of an unhealthy relationship. It is incumbent upon each of us to recognize the problem and take action to change the dynamics and write a new ending. Many of the same healing behaviors can be used here as well, but let's add to them.

- Figure out the roots behind the actions. If your parents were addictive, compulsive, emotionally absent, abusive (fill in the blank), what was the root behind that behavior? Bitterness can manifest itself in a number of unhealthy behaviors, but each is still bitterness. Every

negative emotion may mask itself in a variety of unhealthy behaviors, and breaking the cycle requires recognizing the root and self-treating. Search this out.
- Close the circle. It is not necessary to face someone to close the circle. Sometimes just writing what *you would say* is as effective as having it out face to face. What is important is having that all-important conversation in one way or another. It ends one chapter and opens a blank page for the rest of your life.
- Make a list of opposite behaviors you want to cultivate. These intentional acts change everything.

Once you are sure you've covered the basics, consider other reasons why you may be making bad choices.

Sometimes you are such an optimist that you just fail to see the negative in plain sight. If you are perpetually a glass half full or overflowing kind of person, slow down. Ask yourself questions before making a choice. Ask for the insight of a more cautious or discerning friend. Understand that you have a blind spot and learn to readjust the mirror to avoid making that same mistake over and over again.

Sometimes you are distracted and fail to make appropriate comparisons between two options. These glitches in life happen to all of us. Accept it and move on. Live and learn. If you see this happening to you on a regular basis, however, take some action. Take your time before making a choice. Look at each option for two full minutes. Notice five things about each option before making a choice. These actions preclude snap decisions and offer a better chance of avoiding buyer's remorse.

Sometimes your mental processes short wires. You may know better, but prior experiences blind you to the worth or danger of a particular choice. It's called anchoring bias. Your past hardwired some prejudices into your brain. When you encounter someone with similar characteristics, your brain goes from observation to clanging warning bells. It's not the best way to make a decision. Conversely, if you enjoyed the company of a talkative friend in the past, you may feel drawn to someone who is also a good conversationalist, ignoring other characteristics.

Newton's first law of motion enters the scene here. Sir Isaac Newton postulated three laws for physical motion. First was his realization that a body in motion will not change or slow its motion unless it is met with an equal or greater opposing force. Think of your life as sometimes careening around a curve at breakneck speed. It's dangerous, and you are making bad decisions. You will continue along that same destructive path until an opposing force is applied.

You must be that opposing force. Your strength of will, your reasoning, your ability to change has to be the force that changes the trajectory of a dangerous curve and keeps you safe. You can make the necessary changes from a life of poor choices to a life brimming with good choices.

Chapter Summary

Bad choices may have dotted the landscape of your life in the past, but it doesn't have to be a life sentence. You can change, and your life can benefit from making good choices instead.

- Trauma in your past is often responsible for current bad choices. Heal yourself.
- Break the cycle of destructive choices by recognizing how you have been deceived in the past.
- If you don't take action, nothing will change. You must want to change and save yourself in the process. Others can help, but ultimately all change comes from within.

In the next chapter, you will learn how your choices affect others.

7
YOUR CHOICES INFLUENCE OTHERS

*"Blessed is the influence of one good, loving
human soul on another."*

— George Eliot

Sometimes we forget how interrelated we are, and other times it comes crashing down on us. Nothing has brought that more forcibly to the forefront than varying responses to the COVID-19 pandemic. Let's put politics aside. Let's ignore individual summations. Let's just look at human interactions.

Social media has exploded with information from researchers, doctors, competing authors, and armchair virologists. Everyone can find someone to corroborate one's personal beliefs. So let's just look at the quality of interaction.

I have not seen a nastier period in human exchange than we have experienced in the last three months. It's like our world has exploded with a proliferation of unkind words, unfriending, and blocking destroying many friendships.

The choices many are making define themselves. They also affect others. Now realize that *books* are written on these topics. We are skimming the surface, and it's my job to refine the tomes of literature into a chapter you can read and assimilate as it relates to you and your choices. So right now, just forgive my brevity.

Social Media. The proliferation of online discourse makes everything seem like it is spoken in bold tones. Your choices become much more important in terms of the number of people who see your posts, who interact with you, and whose opinions are molded by what you share online. You can stir up feelings of anger or kindness, but your posts are rarely emotionally neutral.

Remember that misunderstandings are rife in online communication. Your typed words are not accompanied by either verbal or nonverbal cues. Be quick to pick up the phone if your choice of words has been misunderstood. It doesn't matter who is at fault. You see a problem. Choose to fix it!

Write, review, delete if necessary, spellcheck, think about it, and *then* post. This chain of events makes your communication one of clear, intentional thought, well communicated, and hopefully well received. You are the mirror for social acceptance, so be a good role model in what you put out there.

Group Behavior. I remember well a study described in an auditorium full of college students. Deer, the most benign animals in the forest (because we all loved Bambi), were allowed to populate without control on a small island. After a while, researchers were amazed as deer began to behave in very un-deerlike behaviors of aggression. Stressors change group norms or values.

This is seen in mobs and riots. Individuals who would

never, left alone, deface a building will stand by or participate in group behaviors of destruction. Individual conscience is overwritten by the collective conscience, and aggressive behaviors are accepted.

Individual Responsibility. It, therefore, rests upon you to decide, right here and right now, your own personal belief system. Your actions, your choices, affect many more people than just yourself. As you codify your own values, it becomes a frame of reference in your choices of future behaviors. When your choices reflect your values, you sense the integrity of your actions. When your choices do not, the dissonance creates a mental checking point. You can override your instinctive check, but the result most often is one of regret. Learn how to stop. Think. Act rather than react. These are the choices you'll find most rewarding.

Adolescent usage of social media has skyrocketed. Current events are rocking our news feeds. It can be arguably understood that social pressure and examples affect us as never before. That you are taking responsibility for your choices and influence is a tremendous step forward, so let's talk about what that means.

We all have incidents in the past that we wish we could erase, but we are more than a software application. We cannot erase words once spoken nor remove incidents from the minds of others. Take a moment to look back. Are there moments you wish you could revisit? The good news is, you can. Part of moving forward with integrity includes looking backward with responsibility.

When our choices have hurt another person, it is important to consider offering an apology. It is not always possible or advisable, as much depends on the framework of the offended party, but a *willingness* to address personal wrongs indicates personal growth on your own part. My suggestion is a simple one: Write down the incident. Describe your personal choice and how it affected another. Express your own regret. Then, burn it. What I'm suggesting is a clearing of the debris in your own mind. Further actions are beyond the scope of my ability to advise you. But begin. Take personal responsibility for yourself, to yourself.

This may seem like an artificial exercise, but there's nothing fictional about the memories you harbor nor the guilt you may sense rippling under the surface of your consciousness. The past affects both the present and the future, so let's give you a fresh beginning.

This exercise can take an hour or a month. Take your time. The object is a fresh start, not smearing of the mud on the windshield of your soul. Your good friend, your journal, will help with this. The cathartic effect of letting the past go is an enormous boon to good mental health.

Moving Forward. Now it's time to hone in on your personal code of ethics, the basis by which you choose your actions going forward in life. These become your everyday rules of living, interacting with others. Write them down in your journal and take a week to review them. Reflect on their order. Reword them as necessary. The idea is to choose what you believe.

The last step is defining those behaviors that reflect each rule. This is critical. You may choose to edify those you meet, casually, and within your circle of friends. Does that mean you smile at others? Greet others? Offer meaningful dialogue? Offer reproof when necessary? These are all edifying behaviors, but not all of these behaviors feel appropriate. Learning how to live by your beliefs is a lifelong quest.

When you feel you've failed, go back through the process. Write about it. Let it go. Review the value you feel you ignored. What are the acceptable behaviors? In the process, you become the person you want to be, and your values are congruent with your choices.

Influence. It is within you to do much good, and most often, it will be done in small ways. Few of us will end up as typical leaders, heads of government, or in charge of industrial complexes, but hundreds of lives touched these leaders. Each *touch*, a life brushing against another, exerted an influence on the person the leader became.

Being a citizen on planet earth means learning how to influence for good. It involves kind words, charitable acts, giving, and serving. Write down a list of individuals you see on a somewhat regular basis. That is your sphere of influence. Draw a circle. Place a dot in the center. Now draw three concentric circles around that dot. The first circle represents people you see daily. The second circle represents people you see weekly. The third circle represents the lives you touch on social media. Place dots or initials along or within each circle.

You have an opportunity to influence each person in those circles. The main way we do that is through our communication, verbal and nonverbal. To make the most of these opportunities, show up. Be intentional. Be in the moment. Speak affirming words. Realize that typical positions of authority are like lightning rods, attracting killer strikes of fire from clouds around us. Influence accomplishes so much more with very little danger or effort. Be an influencer.

The average person will touch 80,000 lives throughout a lifetime. Whoa! That's a lot of people. What if those represent 80,000 random acts of kindness? Make a list in your journal of kind acts you could perform for others, and work on doing one a day. Then two a day. Then make kindness a habit. Frank Capra's classic *It's a Wonderful Life* demonstrates visually just how many lives one person touches. The influence you exert will return to you. I promise.

Self-Care. Some of your most important choices and how they impact others will come from the behaviors involved in your own self-care. Many of the people around you suffer from low self-worth. When they observe the way you take care of yourself—grooming, appropriate rest, time for reflection, time for self-improvement—the message is not lost on those around you. They learn, and bit by bit, they offer you the sincerest form of praise: they emulate your healthy behaviors.

Remember to fill your own cup, so you have more to give to others. Sometimes decisions should be made with the best interest of the self in mind, accepting and understanding that it will play a part in the lives of others too. Other times, make decisions based on others' needs. Though difficult, it is beneficial to consider others and think less of oneself. It's a delicate balance, isn't it? Acknowledging that each choice made will affect another person is a valuable way to live, not only with the big things but also with small decisions. Choices matter. People matter. Use your influence for good.

Chapter Summary

Influence, simply put, is an indirect influence in the actions of others around you. You will influence more people than you *lead* in life. Your life choices make a difference.

- Social media has become a huge source of influence. Make your feed a source of positive influence.

- Make sure your choices in groups reflect your personal values. Speak up and stand up for what you believe.
- Your influence is the sum total of all the ways your life brushes up against others. Your choices determine what kind of influence you exert.

In the next chapter, you will learn why a crystal ball is not the best medium for making good choices.

8

THE ENIGMA OF THE CRYSTAL BALL

"The magic is inside you. There ain't no crystal ball."

— Dolly Parton

THE VINTAGE MAGIC 8 BALL IS A GREAT TOY FOR CHILDREN. The black ball is filled with some kind of gel, and triangles swirl around inside of it. Each child gets to ask a question and tip the orb until the answer floats to the surface. Sigh. Life feels so simple with a Magic 8-type crystal ball, doesn't it?

We grow up, however, and we realize there is no crystal ball. There are no easy answers out there to advise us whether to have Chinese or Italian for supper, whether to buy a Jeep or a Camaro, or even whether to wear a suit or dress casually. Options swirl around us, demanding choices, and it can be exhausting and just a tad scary, right? Listen, I'm here to tell you it doesn't have to be.

Inherent in many of life's choices are multiple good options, multiple right paths. You aren't going to mess up your life forever with these preferences. A preference isn't a life path, so lower the scale of the attached drama. Lighten up. I want to share with you some strategies that eliminate the need for a crystal ball.

Face the Unknown. Uncertainty is part of the tapestry of life. It makes choices tricky, and one important part of experiencing peace is facing the unknown and spitting into the wind, so to speak.

Be a tightrope walker. One way to look at the unknown is to figure out a new way of handling the situation. For example, a family member is facing emergency surgery, but your child has a little league game. How can you plan on being both places at once? This is where your backup contingencies come into play. Plan for rides. Assign a picture taker or videographer. Make sure the hospital has you on speed dial. These coping mechanisms embrace the unknown with ways to handle any crisis.

This method is based on balance. Imagine a circus performer walking on a wire without a safety net. Pretty scary, huh? The safety net allows the artist to bounce across the wire without fear of calamity, and that's exactly how contingency plans are supposed to function. You can prepare for the unknown far ahead of time by building a support network. Be part of a co-op sharing rides. Watch for friends and neighbors with needs and help out; you'll be needing a favor one day yourself. This mental outlook is your way of making sure a safety net is always available.

Be a lion tamer. Have you ever watched a lion tamer wielding a whip and a chair? The tamer survives by employing fast reflexes to adapt to whatever the lion does. The lion rears up? The chair goes up. Does the lion slink around the cage? The whip forces it back. Adaptation to the vagaries of the unknown is a lot like being a lion tamer.

Adaptation requires quick thinking and flexibility. It means you know what to do in any given situation and can adjust your routine as necessary. To become a lion tamer, list your regular responsibilities, and then decide on how to make decisions. Meal planning, a social calendar, business obligations, and budgetary choices all fall easily within the realm of adapting to what comes your way.

Be a ringleader. Who calls out the performers and plans the program at the circus? The ringleader reserves the right to call out an act when they are good and ready, and marshals the troop for each performance. You can choose to reserve judgment in any situation. You can choose to decide tomorrow. You can choose to decide on the spur of the moment.

One way to handle the unknown is to marshal your resources and choose when to make a decision. Take a moment to gather facts and assess the situation. 99.9% of all decisions are *not* life and death. It's okay to breathe.

How does each of these strategies play out in facing the unknown? Let's look at a simple situation and examine the response of each. Suppose you just found out your supervisor is being canned, and you will be getting a new boss. Your current supervisor has been so much more than a boss, a friend, and a mentor as well. Conflicting loyalties, the need for consistent income, moral obligations...a host of responses are possible. And who knows if you'll like the new boss, if you'll still enjoy working for the company, or if you can get a job on the spur of the moment? To stay or to go? Ack! The uncertainty!

The tightrope walker would find a way to balance the relationship with the need for a steady paycheck. Keep every option open, balance on the narrow beam of life. The lion tamer would adapt to the change. Duck any fallout.

Wish your boss well and get ready to batten down the hatches. The ringleader would be proactive. Visit HR and talk about the qualities you'd love to see in a new manager, send out some resumes, assume control of the situation.

There is no one right way to respond to the unknown, but there is a way that will feel right to you. Surprisingly, you may have elements of both the lion tamer and the tightrope walker in your makeup, or maybe you've added your ringleader tendencies into the mix as well. Realizing you have strategies at your disposal makes life a lot more comforting, though, doesn't it?

Plan ahead. Life coaches have detailed the most difficult choices before you, and it's no surprise that these choices are coming your way. By looking ahead, pondering, and investigating options, you can forestall much of life's angst. Let's look at these categories:

- Several revolve around education and careers. Go wide. For example, the technological landscape is evolving rapidly. Some great opportunities are not yet available. What you *can* do is focus on areas of interest. Choose a broad category like engineering and choose a good school to keep options open. You may discover palatable choices along the way that you simply cannot predict. Go wide.
- Several big choices revolve around life. A companion, a home, a family may all be unknowns at the present time. Prepare ahead of time by knowing the type of companion you would love to find. List qualities you hope to find. Be cognizant of the lifestyles around you. The idea of a home in the country may sound idyllic,

but do you like to mow the grass? A lot of it?
Many of your choices in life are predicated on
what you already know about yourself. Take time
to think things through.

One of the most crippling forms of choice revolves around one simple choice you will make over and over again. Do you know when to quit? A job, a relationship, a home...you begin many things by falling in love with a choice, but all choices proceed through a predictable timeline. Infatuation dies away. Suddenly the pluses and minuses require you to look at your choice in the face. Ultimately you must decide when to move on, and it can be fraught with angst.

Knowing when to quit anything is a personal choice you must make over and over again. Choose wisely, and feel grateful for the opportunity that was yours. Choose poorly, and experience regret or bitterness. Certain behaviors offer you answers. Are you venting a lot? Is it affecting your health? Is dread a constant companion? It may be time to quit. Unfortunately, these are solitary decisions. You can talk through your conflicting emotions with a life coach and seek counsel from someone who knows you well, but you and you alone will live with the consequences of the choice you make.

The best coaches offer this advice:

- Don't be hasty.
- Think it through from several perspectives.
- Who else is affected by this choice?
- Is my choice going to hurt someone I love?
- What is my responsibility in this situation?
- Can I quit with my self-respect intact?

Life is uncertain, and I get it. Like you, I've often wished I had a crystal ball to tell me what to do, but the unknown simply is and will remain unknown. Your best way to face the unknown is to recognize the best coping strategies and learn to enjoy the ride.

Chapter Summary

Life is understood by looking backward but lived by looking forward. I hope you'll take time to think about the strategies offered in this chapter because fear of the unknown is no way to live. You can avoid that stress.

- Figure out if you're a tightrope walker, a lion tamer or a ringleader. If you have all three within you, figure out which one you have been when difficult situations have required a choice between unknown outcomes. Learn how and when to react.
- Plan ahead for many of life's choices. This isn't rocket science.
- Know when to quit. Quit on your terms with your self-respect intact.

In the next chapter, you will learn the differences between choices and decisions, and the impact of each on your life.

9

THE DIFFERENCES BETWEEN CHOICES AND DECISIONS

"Little choices determine habits. Habits carve and mold character, which makes the big decisions."

— ELIZABETH GEORGE

UP TO NOW, WE'VE BEEN FOCUSED ON CHOICE. IT'S AN interesting word, isn't it? It implies options; it implies a one time option of one thing over another. What to eat for breakfast one morning is a choice. A resolve not to eat sugary cereal for breakfast is a decision. Do you see from this little snippet the difference between choice and decision?

- A decision is like a sign at a trailhead. It marks the beginning of your trek and signals the path you're on. It points the way and commits you to a new path.
- A decision has embedded within it the realization that you have made a choice, and that

choice is so much bigger than a one-time flight of fancy.
- Choosing a breakfast cereal is an act of volition. You have multiple choices and are able to pick one. A decision to remove sugary cereals is an outcome of many days of healthful eating.
- Choice is personal. You, just you, get to select one cereal. It's based on emotional attachment, with some reasoning thrown into the mix. Decisions are more cognitive and less emotional.

Through the rest of this book, we will be embarking on the trek of making decisions. Your goal is to make thoughtful, reasoned, congruent decisions in directing your path. For some people, indecisive angst rules the day. We'll talk about that. No decision *is* a decision. We'll talk about that, too. Some wander down the paths of least resistant or instant gratification. There's a problem with that, and we'll course correct.

It's fitting that we discussed choice first. The act of being in touch with your emotions and learning to make a choice is a bedrock part of every decision. You need to decide, for example, on a career major. It is (to coin a pun) a major decision in your life. It comes down to a series of choices that culminate in a decision. We're going to talk about some of these major complex decisions and learn how to break them down into manageable day trips. In the end, you make a choice, but the decision-making process is what steers you into making the best possible choice.

A choice without decision brings no lasting pleasure. Let's compare two types of choices made without deliberation. First, the choice of what to eat for breakfast. You make a choice on Monday morning, but Tuesday morning presents you with the same options, the same requisite choice. It becomes a daily act of volition and never ends...until you decide on a dietary regimen without sugar. Suddenly the decision frees you and brings you a sense of wellbeing, a sense of contentment. Okay, that's simple. What about a more complex choice?

You need to decide on your major for college. So many options! How to decide with so little information? You look at the advertisements for job openings and see that one option offers a lot of opportunities and a great paycheck, so boom! Your choice is made. You will become a CRNA (certified registered nurse anesthetist). One year later, you discover that you faint at the sight of blood. Oops! The choice made without adequate deliberation was a big mistake. Choice without decision, without reasoned deliberation, can only take you so far.

So here's to the rest of the journey. Make a list of big life decisions ahead of you. They can be personal. It's okay if they revolve around work or play...but make that list. Choose one to use as your focus as we continue. Apply each of the forthcoming chapters as part of the process as you deliberate on your options and make a decision that brings you peace of mind. See for yourself how valuable it is to make reasoned, congruent decisions. This is where I will serve as your life coach and help you along the way.

Every trail guide knows where to break for camp each day, what pitfalls lie ahead, and the best way to reach the destination. Trust me as I take you on this journey. Like others before you, you will become one of the select who know how to make decisions you are proud of, decisions others respect. Let's do this together, shall we?

Chapter Summary

A choice implies a single act of volition between a number of options, but a decision implies setting a course in which your choices become part of the framework of who you are and the matrix of your life's story.

- Decisions need to factor in all the nuances that will affect you now and in the years to come.
- Decisions need to be congruent, or in other words, in line with your values and your core set of beliefs.
- A decision is life-changing. It implies direction and purpose and destination.

In the next chapter, you will learn what happens when to avoid or put off an important decision. Sometimes it's okay to say, "No, no, no!"

PART II

THE UNIVERSE OF DECISION

10

WHEN YOUR BRAIN GOES TO WORK

"When I look at the human brain, I'm still in awe of it."

— Ben Carson

Most of us live in this merry little world where choices, decisions, life just happens! Actually, nothing could be further from the truth. The human body dedicates special sections of the brain for the duty of decision making, and it's surprising that so few people discuss this. For many years scientists believed the hippocampus, an obscure part of the brain responsible for memories, was the hot spot for making decisions. That was important, because the hippocampus was part of the limbic system, and it was a part of the brain reason seldom invaded. That meant choices were the result of primal urges, and no one could do much about them.

In that construct, logic held no place. While it is true that logic defies many of our behaviors and often seems to take a back seat, it isn't written in stone. Technology proved that untrue.

Researchers used an MRI (Magnetic Resonating Image) to study people with addictions being exposed to their cravings. Imagine the whispers of astonishment when a part of the cerebral cortex lit up with the suggestion of a cigarette to someone with nicotine addiction. Suddenly a whole new appreciation for the role of deliberate decision making entered into the discussion of hopeless addictions. What if smoking that next cigarette isn't a choice, but rather, a decision? Suddenly the human race has been given a second chance to determine its own destiny.

The thinking part of our brain can be taught how to make better decisions, and you have a part to play in the decisions your brain is making for you. You are not a hapless victim in the process, but an active participant.

Neuroscience took a huge step forward with that understanding, but time stands still for no man. Continuing research has given us additional insights:

- You probably know about the right and left brain, the realization that each side of the brain promotes certain functions, and that we are primarily right or left-brained has been an interesting side note to the study of the mind. When it comes to decision making, however, it makes little difference. Both sides work together in making a decision.
- As it turns out, the hippocampus does indeed play a part in decision making, pulling memories into the equation. Your brain sets up a thread of connections tying together information from the cerebral cortex of the left brain, the right brain,

and the hippocampus to make a split-second
analysis for many of the decisions you make
each day.

Continuing research spanning more than thirty years involved mind-mapping of the functions of the cerebral cortex. Scientists studied the function of patients with brain injuries, and in the process, learned where each function is housed within the brain. In the course of their research, they realized that decision making does indeed light up several parts of the brain. A lesion in one part of the cerebral cortex hampers decision making for that individual, and the deficiency can last forever.

Further research led by Max Planx at the Institute for Human Cognitive and Brain Science revealed a startling hypothesis. The brain makes hundreds of decisions a day, and in each one, the impulse to act on the decision is sent out before the individual even realizes they've made a decision. These routine, almost instantaneous decisions are a product of your memory taking action, relieving the cerebral cortex of the responsibility to chime in or help in the process. "Do you take your coffee with cream or sugar?" You answer without thinking. Your brain already knows your answer.

Many of these automatic responses are behavior-driven; you could almost call them reflexes. They aren't embedded over centuries but cultivated by behavioral responses your brain has learned to decipher from past interactions. Marketers have a field day with this aspect of personal conditioning, and it's always important to contemplate on what seems like second nature. Are these the values you want? You have the power to keep or change these impulses, but always, it's you. Other powers may influence you, but you choose to listen, to buy, to believe. Take ownership of your mind and assume self-control. As you do, you will realize you have successfully conditioned your own mind, and the need for conscious choice or decision in some areas no longer exists.

Does this relieve you of responsibility in complex, important decisions? Sadly no. You are required to put in the work to make a good decision, but realizing how the decisions are made is helpful. Consciously apply the various contributions your brain makes. Knowing your brain considers decision making a team effort, employ all the members of the team!

- Be rational. Think of the significant points of each option. Reason things out.
- Use your memory. What correlations can you make from past experience?
- Be emotional. What is your gut reaction to each option?

Recognize the impact of those around you. Inherent in personal responsibility is the requirement that each of us self-examines our responses to be sure they are just that —*our own responses.* Sometimes our tribes dictate basic values and our resultant decisions. When that happens, the herd mentality leads to less autonomy, even as we feel good about our choices. Political affiliations, ethnic culture, and societal norms all exert pressure to form and mold us. A thinking person must take those so-called intrinsic beliefs and expose them to the light of day, must consciously accept or reject each one, and then choose congruent behaviors. Doing so provides a personal framework and code of conduct. It requires mindfulness.

A study on mindfulness revealed that applying just fifteen minutes of conscious thought to any decision improves the outcome. Think of the best-case scenarios. Think of the worst-case scenarios. Ask yourself if you have considered every aspect of the decision. Those fifteen minutes separate the Rockefellers from the homeless person on the street. One has learned how to make effective decisions. The other has not.

Chapter Summary

Not surprisingly, our complex brains never take a day off. They remain busy compiling information and making decisions for us, allowing us to enjoy being on autopilot for a while each day. Also not surprising, we can access the parts of the brain that participate in decision-making, and actively intervene to make better decisions.

- The brain is rational. Think about the implications of a decision before you decide.
- The brain is hardwired with connections to your storeroom of life's memories. Think of past experiences and the nuances of each decision before you make a decision. Apply reason, emotion, and intellect. Look forward and backward. This conscious *knowing* gives you the assurance you can trust the decision you made.
- The brain is emotional. Never disregard how you feel as you decide.

In the next chapter, you will learn what happens when you avoid or put off an important decision.

11

AVOIDANCE...NO DECISION IS A DECISION

"Cats are dangerous companions for writers, because cat-watching is a near perfect method of writing avoidance."

— Dan Greenberg

What are the ways you speak avoidance? Here are a few. Do you *stall* when a difficult decision paralyzes you? Stalling implies putting it off, maybe dancing from foot to foot as if the ground is too hot to stand on. Stalling feels weak, doesn't it? What about the word *evade*? It's like dodging a bullet. The word is seldom used in a positive connotation. People evade their taxes, criminals evade capture, and rooted inside the word is a hint of desperation. Evading arrest just postpones the inevitable. Every lawbreaker has their day in court. Do you like the word *ignore*? It means you know you have to decide at some point, but you ignore it for the time being. Do you suppose that brings you any extra peace of mind? It hangs over you all the while.

In professional terms, it is called avoidance. It implies all of those actions: stalling, evading, ignoring, and all it does is postpone a date with destiny. Most of the time, when we avoid a decision, it is because it involves recognized or subsurface conflict. Professionals refer to conflict-avoidance as an almost pathological refusal to consider any decision that engenders negativity, but bits of it lurk within all of us. Perhaps you feel caught between two people in making a big decision, a decision that will incur the displeasure of one of those two most valued people in your life. So you hesitate, and here's the catch: Avoiding the decision creates a wound all its own.

If you were a mouse in the corner of this giant computer we call your brain, you'd see it humming on a regular basis, a vast conglomerate of neural junctions and pathways crossing over, intersecting, originating, and ending at various ports. Of course, this is just a caricature of the way the brain looks and works, but it gets the point across. If you look closer, you'd see some parts are pathways without end terminals. These represent the unresolved conflicts that affect your decision-making process. Most are buried beneath the surface of daily functions. Some are so long forgotten that you could hardly define the point of origin if you tried.

Yet the debris of all these unresolved conflicts doesn't just disappear because you stopped thinking about them. They clutter up your mind and wait to be resolved. We aren't talking about a couch and psychotherapy here. It's much easier than that.

Think of a decision you've been procrastinating. Who will be disappointed by your decision, one way or the other? Now settle down with a piece of paper and a pen. Think of times when you've felt this way before. Keep thinking. Go back to memories from your formative years. As you do, you'll see a pattern emerge. The genesis of your avoidance can be traced to one of several primal emotions:

- Shame—you, at some point, started feeling blame when a decision wasn't accepted by someone else.
- Guilt—this is different from shame. You feel guilty because you didn't want to make a decision someone else wanted.
- Loneliness—you at some point got rejected when a decision wasn't accepted by someone else.
- Pain—you were hurt when someone didn't accept a decision.

Symptoms that you avoid conflict like the plague include piling up or gunnysacking resentments, fear of displeasing others, bitterness from silent resentment, and fear of ridicule when speaking up. Understand that these are not *wrong* feelings; they are just not helpful. Once you recognize what you're doing, it is a lot easier to remedy your situation. The practical application helps you eliminate these subconscious hesitations.

- Practice giving an unwanted decision in front of the mirror. Be sure you know what to say.
- Practice tempering unpleasant decisions with phrases of affirmation.
- Start with small decisions or conflicts and move into the more difficult ones with practice.
- Express your ability to empathize with another's position.
- Show your compassion for the distress your decision may cause.

- Dream up some pluses that may be appreciated.
- Affirm your respect and affection.

What happens when you continue to avoid making a decision? Realize that *not making a decision IS a decision.* When two competing activities force you to make a difficult decision, and you avoid making it to prevent anyone from being displeased, you end up missing both events and displeasing both parties. That may not be the best course of action. You are offered an opportunity for extra work in the office. You promise to consider it, but are conflicted between the time it takes from your after hour pleasures and how much money it actually adds to your paycheck...but at the same time, saying, "No, thanks" doesn't feel like an acceptable option. You avoid making a decision. *That is a decision, and it doesn't add any respect to your stature.* A boss chalks it up to poor manners, unprofessional conduct, or an unwillingness to be a team player. Is that what you wanted to communicate?

When you typically avoid making decisions, you often rather conveniently forget you have a decision to make. Let's be honest here. You probably shoved it down on your radar to a point where it never surfaced again. Be proactive by starting a column in your planner for decisions you need to make or action that needs to be taken. Assign a due date. Review it weekly and respond in a timely way.

The sneaky thing about avoidance is the way it sabotages you in both your personal and professional relations. Remember, you're not doing yourself any favors by procrastinating or avoiding decisions...quite the opposite.

Chapter Summary

Avoiding a decision is a decision in and of itself, leaving an impression you may not want to be making. Avoidance is often related to past disappointments, but you are not bound by those. You have the power to change.

- Think about why you are avoiding decisions. Understand yourself and then make a decision to change.
- Learn how to offer unpleasant decisions more palatable. Practice giving affirmations.
- Develop a system for tracking decisions you need to make and set a time each week to make sure you are doing so in a timely way.
- Even when the data seems insufficient and the path unclear, decide to choose. Always decide to choose.

In the next chapter, you will learn how to stand tall in the face of fear.

12

NO FEAR!

*"Too many of us are not living our dreams
because we are living our fears."*

— Les Brown

With all the reality TV, you'd think fear would have vacated the premises by now, but don't bet on it. We like to see others conquer their fears, but it's a vicarious pleasure producing no fruits within. Decision making, especially the big ones, is *just as scary*. There's a word for it: decidophobia, the fear of making decisions. Let's separate this into two parts. The usual fear we all feel in the heat of the moment, and the crippling fear when it dominates our lives.

Fear in the Moment. If you're a baseball fan, it's like two-out, bases loaded, the game tied, and a slugger comes up to bat. Each pitch is a nailbiter because there's no rerun or back up when it comes to consequences. Each decision on where to place the ball wins or loses the game. Each decision to swing is fraught with angst.

When it comes to choosing a college major, buying a house, taking a job, or choosing a companion, those same stakes come into play. A major league pitcher hurls a fastball at more than ninety miles per hour, traveling to the plate in 375–400 *milliseconds*! It takes lightning-quick reflexes to decide whether to swing and where the ball may be crossing the plate.

You may have known a decision was coming, but hey, if you procrastinated at all, it's suddenly upon you. Perhaps you've given it some attention, but after studying it, find you are no closer to a decision. Wait! The pitcher is winding up, and the ball is about to be hurled straight at you! What are you going to do? You have no crystal ball and no promise it will turn out okay. That pressure is debilitating for many of us...but it doesn't need to be.

Fear is a primal emotion, embedded within us with the release of adrenaline, the fight or flight hormone, whenever that decision is pitched our way. The physical manifestations include sweating, a pounding heart, and a dry mouth. You know them well. No one in their right mind would counsel you to ignore those warning bells.

Just remember this: Fear is not your enemy. It's your warning that something big is about to happen. Let me give you a few hints.

- First of all, you may be surprised to discover the decision has already been made. By studying the issues ahead of time, your mind has weighed the evidence, and it's just been waiting for the right moment to fill you in. Suddenly you blurt out a decision that surprises even yourself! Score!
- Second, realize that we have managed to survive

on this planet precisely because of this response to danger. If the pitcher is winding up and all you feel is fear, step away from the plate. Let the pitcher stew while you take a deep breath, marshal your resources, and then get ready to hit it out of the park.
- Third, learn to recognize the difference between generalized anxiety and fear. Anxiety denotes a tendency to overthink a minor decision, as opposed to fear that results from leaning in the wrong direction over a complex decision. One can be controlled; the other should be listened to and evaluated.

Decidophobia. An overwhelming fear of all decisions is crippling. How do you know for sure if this is affecting you? I think you already know, deep down inside, but here are some warning signs: You avoid all decisions, even the easy ones. Every decision fills you with dread. You look for help...from a friend or the stars...anything to avoid taking responsibility for the decision by yourself. The anxiety is crippling. A decision of eggs or pancakes for breakfast leaves you feeling spent. I know that sounds trivial, but it isn't for some.

Overcoming that paralysis is well within your abilities. First, decide to decide. The more trivial decisions you make, the easier it becomes to make larger decisions. Plot out the "what ifs" for best and worst-case scenarios. If you can live with the worst case, it suddenly doesn't matter. If you must have the best-case scenario, play it safe.

Some of your self-healing comes from visiting with a friend. Learn to see things from the perspective of someone you respect. That grounding can be emulated and practiced until you, too, feel no fear.

Try writing out your reasoning and analyzing the aftereffects. Ask questions and look at the facts. Categorize decisions as major wins, major losses, or nonessential. I think you'll find that much of what fills you with anxiety doesn't really bother you at all. This should remove some of that fear. This is especially helpful in decisions over large purchases. A handy rule in our household is to spend as much time in research over purchases as it took to earn the money for those purchases. Taking time to reflect and research removes a lot of the angst.

Game Seven of the World Series. Let's go back to the biggest decisions of all. There is no denying the importance of major life decisions, each bearing an impact for years or generations to come. The weight of those decisions feels very heavy indeed. I want to encourage you to face them head-on.

- Initiate the pre-game analysis. Every hitter watches tapes of the opposing pitchers and studies ahead of time. You can as well. Begin by taking the time to analyze the decision. Remember that your brain will continue to study the topic while you're off getting peanuts at the ball game. That's okay.
- Visualize a home run. See the future as a win. Let your mind follow suit.
- Get ready to swing. A swing begins with some backward motion. The bat is drawn back so it can swing forward with maximum velocity. Review your past. Know what has affected you, what you long for, and what you need.

- Swing hard. You might as well hit it out of the park. No ribbons are awarded to half-hearted swings.
- Follow through. The batter swings the bat even after connecting with the ball. That means you have to commit yourself to run to the bases. Do the work. Make it a success.

Life throws many decisions at you in the course of a day, and in learning to handle the little things gracefully, you'll find yourself better prepared for the big decisions sure to come your way. A lifetime of preparation goes into making these big decisions, which become the basis and structure of where you live, how you live, and with whom. But rather than dreading them, look forward to the opportunity! You are the hero in your own life story, and you get to make the game-winning run. Do so with style!

Chapter Summary

Decisions are not for the faint of heart. It is hard, and I won't deny that. But I will say that you have within yourself all you need to make better decisions with less anxiety. When you learn how to manage your fear—not abolish it—you will find yourself much more comfortable in all the big decisions of life.

- Remember that your brain works for you. Let it be working out the thorny details of a major decision while you're enjoying the game. Ponder on decisions ahead of time.
- Harness your fears to engage all your attention when it is necessary.

- When you are faced with a big decision, give it all you've got.

In the next chapter, we will learn what and how to F-O-C-U-S.

13

FOCUS, FOCUS, FOCUS

"Live life to the fullest, and focus on the positive."

— MATT CAMERON

WE THINK OF BOSSES, CEOS, AND MANAGERS AS BEING problem-solving decision-makers, and they are...but does that mean you can't be one yourself? You are the CEO of your own life, and I want you to feel more empowered than you have in the past in both your ability and the necessity of making good decisions. The good decision I refer to isn't based on its inherent value, but in its representation of your input and congruence with your own values.

Most of the time, as you've discovered, your brain works on autopilot, and that's a good thing. There are those decisions, big life decisions, that require conscious thought. These decisions should be predicated on thought rather than emotion and should be well thought out.

It sounds basic, easy, a no-brainer, right? You'd be surprised at how many lack the ability to focus on making good decisions. Some like to focus on what they want, but desires are fleeting and based on changing situations. Congruent decisions are value-based and are derived from the examination of your own value system.

Let's begin with your personal code of conduct. List ten values you hold to be central to your life. I'll prime the pump with a few obvious examples. A physician holds *do no harm* as a central tenet of patient care. A thief might say *never cheat a partner*, belying the notion of no honor among thieves. Your code of conduct is your most basic, first, and last basis for making a decision. Some options in life are immediately discarded for flagrant violation of all you hold dear, while some choices may survive right down to the wire and then be discarded in the final analysis with the realization they cause a ripple in your conscience.

Your conscience is the residence of this code of conduct. I know, it defies a place in the brain that I can point to and say, "There! Subject choices to the scrutiny of your..." Rather, they represent the sum of your thinking cortex and your limbic hippocampus where experience, memory, and conscious thought meet at an important intersection. You can sear your conscience until its warnings are no longer noticed, but to do so leaves you vulnerable to making the worst of decisions. A damaged conscience can always be reclaimed by the process of going back. List ten values in your personal code of conduct. Make these the basis of all decisions. Once you have done this, decision making becomes a lot less scary. You can proceed through the process assured of a good outcome.

The paralysis of being unable to make a decision can be warded off by employing a simple process over and over again. It becomes easier, almost instinctive, with repeated use of the formula. All it takes is to focus on the important parts of the process. The steps in making a decision include:

- Writing down the decision to be made. This all-important step is the foundation of a good outcome. Fuzzy thinking about what you're trying to decide precludes a horrific ending to the story. Whittle your description down to a single sentence. Do you find that hard? Ask yourself a series of *why* questions. *Why do you need to make a decision?* Be the toddler here, asking why over and over again until you reduce the question down to its most basic core, a simple statement of the issue at hand.
- Compile the data, and I chose that word deliberately. Become a fact magnet. Some lose their ability to make a good decision because it is based on all the wrong assumptions. Contrast that with searching for *facts*. The term "data" denotes something more than generalized impressions, doesn't it? Go big in your analysis.
- Figure out the possible outcomes of this decision. List them all, even if you consider them implausible. Brainstorm other possible outcomes based on your research. Focus is a head game, so use your brain here.
- Assign each possible outcome a probability score. Assess the realities. You can use a plus or minus, or you can assign your own percentage points, but this becomes an important part of your rationale. Think it through.
- Obtain feedback. Sometimes a parent or grandparent or mentor has faced the same decision. Reviewing your thought processes can be valuable. Additional insight may yield

outcomes you had not considered or change the values of outcomes you previously rated.
- Decide. Yup. Stop obsessing and decide.

Focus is your ability to employ your mind for the duration of the process. If you are easily distracted, give each step a ten-minute time limit, step away, and resume after a short break. The key is to not give up partway through the process.

Chapter Summary

This chapter is deliberately short and sweet. I'm giving you a decision-making paradigm that works. Use it!

- There are five basic steps in the decision-making process. Don't try to skip one.
- This paradigm can be used on *every* big decision in your future.
- The more you perform this exercise, the easier it gets.

In the next chapter, you will learn how to reduce life's complex fractions.

14

NARROW DOWN YOUR OPTIONS

"Life is really simple, but we insist on making it complicated."

— Confucius

It seems logical that a complex decision is made easier by narrowing down the options or potential choices involved, but you must apply your finest reasoning to this process.

Let's consider an example. One hapless soul decides to flip a coin when a decision comes down to two possible outcomes. Let's assume this is a simple decision between two flavors of ice cream, and the weight of the world isn't resting in the balance. Okay, it's a 50/50 chance, right? Don't bet on it. Each minted coin holds its own minute dimples and ridges from the minting process. Subtle pressure from a flipping thumb can change the outcome with a very small bias precluding the predicted 50/50 outcome. Naturally, major decisions defy the flip of the coin.

Implicit in this discussion comes a suggestion found in

multiple places in this book because it is just that important. **Begin by refining your decision to one problem or set of options that must be decided between.** All action follows the basic premise that you know your issue and can state it succinctly. Once you have reduced your decision into a bite-sized sentence, begin listing every possible option.

Don't rate or judge any option in this step. Just create the longest, most complete list possible. Not considering the best option is as dangerous as trying to consider too many. Your future best possible solution must be one of the options outlined, so don't skimp on this process. Some people fail to make decisions for fear that better options are out there or will arise. The future isn't your concern. Listing *all* the possible options at this time is your task. Got them? Don't let your fear of the future derail your present. List the options and move on.

Now it's time to narrow the field. Lowering the number of viable options makes a decision not just less painful, but a real possibility. Just as you needed every possible option listed to be sure your future decision was part of the mix, you now need to eliminate the wastage. Some ideas are too frivolous, too expensive, too time consuming, too far out of your value system. That's okay. Gone like the wind! Get this down to two or three of the best options.

Now you can use your prior tool for deciding the best option. Still not sure? Ask yourself some questions as you go through the process. Do I have all the information I need? Do I have the time to consider this now? Are there others I need to consult? What is the first action in each option...does it feel right? I hope you see how this process clarifies and validates your decision.

Studies have shown that too many options can cause depression and anxiety, as indecision paralyzes any forward motion. The only way forward when this happens is through narrowing down all the possible outcomes to the best final choice. Let's look at some specific examples.

A career in 2020 is seldom a choice cemented into your life. The ever-changing landscape of society and interconnectedness of all global industries almost contrive to ensure that most adults will have two or more careers within their lifetimes. Thus, vocation is a major decision for young adults and a recurring decision for many of us. So how do we go about making this all-important choice?

Begin by assessing your interests and natural talents. Every community college and library stocks aptitude tests to help you find your gifts. A lucky few know they love animals and want to work with animals in some form or another, but many from graduate high school unsure of what they want to do. They like a lot of things, and nothing seizes their interest for two years of in-depth study. Seek guidance and assess your traits.

Once you know your strengths, you can begin to narrow things down. You love animals or animal studies, you love human anatomy or human health, you love machines and how they work, you love buildings and how they are designed. See how that works? You have a broad field with a lot of options.

Proceed with the realization that your course of study or career path must be broad enough to adapt to changing circumstances. So if you love animals, don't narrow yourself down to just the study of whales. Move up the continuum to the study of marine wildlife. Does that make sense? It defines your scope of interest without limiting you in any way.

As you continue searching out your perfect future, do some digging on all the options within a given field. For example, marine wildlife can include the study of a single animal, marine biology, care of contained marine life, preservation of endangered marine wildlife...search out these options. List all you can find, then narrow them down to two or three options. These represent a major and a minor or related field of study. This offers you the broadest application within your given field.

Before making a final decision, ask yourself a few more questions: How much training or education is required? Can I afford this option? Does this option restrict my lifestyle in any way, and am I okay with that? Are there transitions within this field, levels of accomplishment, or other variables affecting my employment? Answering these questions refines the options and adds clarity to a difficult decision.

A final caveat is making sure you aren't painting yourself into a corner. This is why many colleges require two years of basic courses before selecting a major. Tastes change. Life has a way of altering your priorities. Deciding, for example, to teach impressionistic art on a graduate level is a narrow career choice, requiring a doctorate level of education. There aren't a lot of easy transitions from that choice halfway through the process into any other career option.

This has been an in-depth review of the process of choosing a career path by narrowing down the options. You've been patient, but a career choice may not be on your radar at all. Maybe you're having trouble deciding on what kind of car to purchase or the best place in town to buy a home. The basics remain the same. Define the problem. List the options. Narrow the options down. Ask questions to clarify your decision.

This process works, but once in a while, you will encounter a roadblock. Competing life requirements, the needs of others, a lack of resources…a myriad of issues can arise to derail your path to a great decision.

What happens when you hit a roadblock in this process? Decision anxiety leads to paralysis. You find yourself afraid to make other decisions, and sadly, soon, it affects your health. We'll cover anxiety in more detail in Chapter 17, but for right now, realize that failure to narrow down the options leads to unhappy outcomes.

Sometimes your decision affects others, and you feel compelled to let others help decide the outcome. The process for a group decision is basically the same. Define the problem. Limit the criteria which can be discussed. Failure to do this leads to day-long meetings and endless frustration. Once everyone involved understands the parameters, list the options, narrow them down, make a decision. What happens if everyone doesn't agree?

Voting ensures some will be happy, and others will be disappointed. If this is a major decision, add an important step. Define the criteria each group cannot live without. It may change the outcome from what you personally consider the *best* option, but group cohesion is maintained if it is the best decision everyone in the group can *live with*, an important distinction.

If you work in any form of management, you need to become an expert at narrowing down the options. You will be faced with many complex decisions and thorny group decisions. Your success rests on eliminating the most egregious options, narrowing the discussion to the best options possible. Your mobility up the career ladder almost guarantees that at some point, you will need to be able to handle complex decisions and remember to narrow down your options. This may not come easily, but it is a skill that can be learned.

Chapter Summary

Most decisions are difficult not because there is no solution, but because there are so many possible outcomes. A good decision requires being able to narrow those options down to just a few worth considering.

- Write down the problem or decision you need to make. Work at this step until it is a simple sentence, and you are satisfied that it's a perfect summation of the situation.
- List every possible option. As you become skilled in the process, you can begin judging some options as they come to mind, but don't take a shortcut until you're sure the best option is in the list.
- Narrow down the options that cost too much, take too much time, or make you feel uncomfortable. Ask yourself questions. As you work through this step, a solution will present itself.

In the next chapter, you will learn how to play the devil's advocate.

15

THE DEVIL'S ADVOCATE

"Every time you are tempted to act the same old way, ask if you want to be a prisoner of the past or a pioneer of the future."

— DEEPAK CHOPRA

SOMETIMES WE JUST DON'T GET IT, RIGHT? We get so caught up in our preconceived notions of what the future *should* look like or what we *think* is right, that we fail to see the forest for the trees. Think about how much easier it would be to make a good decision if you could look at it from a different perspective.

Let's examine this concept for a minute. Go for a walk in a little glen or forest with trees, and observe the landscape around you. Are the trees large or small? Are they all alike? Are they straight or crooked? Look at the bark of the trees and imagine what kind of weather or animal left its mark. Choose one and let it represent your life. Reach up and pluck a leaf. When you have a chance, examine it closely. How many veins does it have, how large is it, is it representative of the other leaves on the tree? Do the leaves attach straight across from each other or at an angle? If you have a magnifying glass, look at it again and see if you glean any more insight.

If that tree represents you, then that one leaf is any given decision you need to make. You see it clearly and know it well, right? What if I told you the opposite is true? What if I told you that you got it all wrong? Plan another outing. Find a hillside from which to view the glen of trees from which you plucked your leaf. Think about the difference in perspective. How many trees are in the little glen...can you count them? Can you identify your individual tree? How many leaves? Is any one leaf able to be distinguished from the others?

If you had to make a decision on the fate of one leaf from a single tree representing your life, would you make that decision from within the forest or from the hillside? One places you intimately into the life of the tree, and the other from a loftier perspective. Is one spot better than the other?

I would submit to you that neither is the place for decision making, but both are essential. Far too often, we make decisions from an emotional vantage point in which all the feels assail us, and we are caught up in the minutia surrounding the issue at hand. That might not be the best place to make a decision. Sometimes we disassociate ourselves from the emotion and people surrounding the situation and try to make a decision from a purely cognitive point of view. Neither one is a correct vantage point all the time, and perhaps not even part of the time.

The best place to make a decision is with full awareness of the tiniest nuances and with a clear broader picture in mind, in a place of contemplation away from the hubris of the situation. Hubris is a funny word, and it connotes an excessive self-assurance. That's exactly what I mean. Approaching these difficult decisions with more than a bit of humility lets us make a better decision.

And just how do we do that? My suggestion is that your decision is intentional, measured, and evaluated. Let's go back to the process in Chapter Twelve and add one more component. Let's add the Devil's Advocate, and let me explain how that might work.

- Write down or understand the issue.
- Collect data.
- Think of options.
- Assign a probability score.
- **Look at the Devil's Advocate.**
- Get feedback.
- Decide.

That simple step of looking at the opposite of the best decision or the aspects of the worst possible outcome in more detail tempers your final decision. It can lead to a better decision...but beware!

An old paper written by the University of Illinois in 1984 and digitalized in 2011 examined the role of the Devil's Advocate in strategic decision making, particularly from a militaristic point of view. President Kennedy's decision at the Bay of Pigs was analyzed. It was determined from studying the puzzle that when a solitary person, in this case, the President of the United States, looks at the viewpoint without sufficient input, it can be disastrous. One additional piece was added to the mix, instituting a devil's advocate approach, and when the Cuban missile crisis unfolded, President Kennedy handled it much better.

It was further observed that when President Johnson tried to employ the same process in determining the course of the Vietnam War, a far different outcome ensued. History would suggest he was comfortable in escalating the conflict *because* he then felt secure in "having heard both sides" of the point of view. The process didn't eliminate decisional error, but rather, cemented a poor decision. That poor decision is the result of a blind spot.

Most of us understand the concept of a blind spot from driving down a road at breakneck speed, deciding to change lanes and getting scared to death when a car hidden in a blind spot lays on its horn. We looked, or at least we thought we did. We started to change lanes very confidently. But hidden from view lay disaster in the form of another car traveling at an equally breakneck speed. A blind spot in decision making can be just as devastating.

That's the value of feedback, time, contemplation. You can uncover your own blindspots and be your own horn of warning. Learning how to do that requires keeping a journal of your thoughts, decisions, and outcomes. It requires learning what happens when you second-guess yourself, when it's effective and when it's not. It comes with experience, and often with age.

Even when you try to employ this step and think you've failed miserably, hindsight may offer you a different perspective. My advice is not to be afraid to add this component to your decision-making process. It will be invaluable in those large complex decisions, and you may develop the knack for employing a part of the process to those rascally fast decisions that pepper your day.

Sometimes life comes at you with all the finesse of a wrecking ball, and you have to make a decision with a lot less preparation. That's when the devil's advocate comes into play. Let's employ just *some* of the basic steps we covered in Chapter Twelve. Know the problem. Think of your options. Choose the best option. Now take a little side trip. What's the opposite of this or the worst that can happen? If you can live with the worst, you can live with the decision. Boom! Done.

These rapid-fire decisions may not be on the scope of where you plan to work or who you plan to marry, but they can be just as impactful when added up and factored into your brain's file cabinet of stored memories. Look at a simple and next to trivial example: A decision to have lunch with a group of gossipy women. Going affects your mindset, which affects your next decision, which affects, ultimately, your major life decisions. It desensitizes you in some ways, predicating continued outings with the same gossipy women, and it inculcates habits that become the character that become your way of life. If you examined the decision from an opposing point of view, would you go to lunch? I hope you see that looking at these little decisions from an opposing viewpoint helps you both today and down the road.

The Devil's Advocacy model is well done within groups, in which one team can critique an option proposed by another group, but it doesn't require a corporate boardroom. It's a lot harder when it's just you invoking the process. Does it make it any less valuable? Nope. Your goal is to learn how to do this and do it quickly. Here are some ideas that may help:

- Find a time when an issue doesn't require a split-second decision. Think or write down the issue, come up with the options, choose one, and then look at the opposite or worst-case

scenario. Do it again and time yourself. That's the time to beat.
- Ask a friend to brainstorm with you if you have trouble coming up with that all-important devil's advocate option for consideration. Some of us find it difficult.
- A few days later, go through this whole experimental process again and time yourself.

Your object is to learn how to make faster decisions as you practice. When life throws you a zinger, and you have to decide how to respond immediately, it will be easier to make a good decision.

Chapter Summary

The Devil's Advocate is a device you can use strategically to make a very large, very considered decision, but with practice, you can employ that same principle to other life situations. It requires a wide lens and some practice, but it's well worth it!

- Use the same decision-making model from Chapter Twelve.
- Learn to look at your decision from both a detailed and broad perspective.
- Ask yourself more questions than usual, and take the side of an opposing point of view.
- Learn to watch for blind spots.

In the next chapter, you will learn what happens when emotion prevails. Will the outcome be good or bad?

16

BE A LION TAMER

"The one excellent thing that can be learned from a lion is that whatever a man intends doing should be done by him with a whole-hearted and strenuous effort."

— CHANAKYA

THINK BACK TO A TIME YOU VISITED THE CIRCUS OR SAW A movie that included a lion tamer. The proverbial image is of a man with a bright suit coat armed with a chair and a whip to hold off a beast with horrific teeth and sharp claws. The lion jumps around the cage, always trying to find a vulnerable spot from which to kill or maim its tamer, but the valiant tamer is ever at the ready.

You have lions in your own life, and they can be just as deadly as the ones in any circus. Those lions are your emotions whipping around you, sometimes overpowering you, always threatening to overcome or destroy you. We talked about the way your subconscious can be alerted to danger with a primal gut instinct, often conjured up and experienced with emotion, but that's not a danger to you in your everyday life. Those premonitions of danger or warning bells occur infrequently and, of course, should not be ignored.

A work published in 1994, *Descartes' Error*, examined what happens when **no** emotion is used in the decision-making process. It debunked the idea that decisions should be made from the colorless vantage point of pure reason. Researchers proved that individuals suffering brain damage, particularly of the prefrontal cortex harvesting emotion, had trouble making any decisions at all! Past experience, much of which is fraught with emotion, clearly plays a part in effective decision making, so don't misunderstand me. I'm not advocating an ascetic life void of emotion. The lions I want you to tame are emotions that have run rampant over the exercise of reason.

What we're examining now are the emotions that can overtake your decision-making apparatus and lead you to disaster. When grief, depression, greed, revenge, lust, or other corrosive emotions override all reason, they become beasts with teeth and claws of their own and may lead to some very regrettable decisions. You can come up with some of these from just thinking about people you've known who offer a classic example of *how **not** to make a decision.* Think of a person who, after a heartbreaking loss, rebounds into a relationship with a cad. Think of a person who suffers the death of a companion and hastily throws things away or sells the house, only to regret it a year later when time has healed the heart. Think of a person who is wronged and passionately lashes out in a way causing physical harm, leading to a stint in prison. Easy to think of examples, isn't it?

Emotions can overrule all reason and overwhelm us. We

- When you get overly emotional, it causes a false sense of security. You feel like you're in control when you may not be, you feel like what you're about to do has to succeed, when in reality, there is every reason to think it won't.
- Realize that many raw emotions are not tidy little feelings, but rather, overarching themes in your life. Your grief or loss may cause you to feel insecure in other areas of your life. The betrayal in one situation may cause you to look for signs of impending doom everywhere. It oozes out and clouds many other parts of your life.

That's why a time of emotional upheaval is precisely the wrong time to make a major decision. It is also why emotions allowed to fester become lions that you have more and more trouble taming. They don't stay in tidy little boxes. Instead, they overwhelm you when you least expect to feel emotional.

Taming those emotions is the work of a lifetime of introspection, reading, processing, and figuring things out. You live during all of that, and decisions come up that won't wait on you. So how do you respond when the lions are all around you? Ah, you have a whip and a chair! Your whip is for identifying the emotion. Your chair is for containment. Here's how it works.

You need to make a decision on whether or not to move from one home or apartment to another, to rent or sell or lease. It's a big decision, but you have to make it. You recognize you are in the throes of adjustment from a big emotion, so first of all, identify the emotions in your soup of messy life. I like to do this with a pen and a piece of paper. I write down the messy emotion and draw a circle of containment around it. If I wasn't grieving, what would I do? If I wasn't madder than a wet chicken, what would I do? If I wasn't feeling the imprint of disloyalty when someone talked about me behind my back, what would I do?

The whip and the chair work for those crisis situations when emotion threatens to overpower us, and a good decision seems impossible. Neither gets rid of the lion, and neither gets it back into the cage. They are survival mechanisms, and it's okay to survive. Survival is a good thing.

Getting the lions back into their cage is a whole other process. It involves time. It takes the willingness to think, and I am so easily distracted, it takes a journal to keep track of the chicken tracks my mind makes all over the landscape. It requires processing the events and emotions until you can distill a life lesson until you can feel the lions slowly slipping into captivity. Those lions don't disappear; they merely cease to threaten you.

A prelude to a circus is often a parade, and you can see lions safely held within their cages, roaring and wanting to escape, but unable to get through those narrow bars, unable to chew the metal surrounding them. Your emotions will eventually be relegated to a safe place in your psyche, and you will be able to view them more dispassionately. They may threaten to overwhelm you, but only if you let them out of their cage.

We never expect them to get loose, but they do, so how do we prepare for their escape? Be aware of what triggers the release of that old emotion. Learn to avoid the triggers. Keep track of when big life events happen. Sometimes a season of the year heralds a remembrance. Try to postpone major decisions. Utilize your whip and chair if you must, and process the old experience until it is caged once again.

Studies were done on neutral subjects given positive or negative stimuli, proving that moods affect outcomes. A positive mood generates a far different decision or outcome than a person feeling negative. If you looked at your life and assigned a value to the positive or negative emotions you feel, you'd find that sometimes those with a higher number override the smaller number. For example, you may feel kindly toward dogs, but passionate arousal of a child being mangled by a pit bull may evoke a different response toward an ordinance banning or allowing pit bulls in the neighborhood. The *degree* of your emotion or feeling affects your decision.

It is also understood that small triggers can affect your emotions and resultant decision making. Researchers found a positive correlation between the numbers in the stock market on sunny days over cloudy days. Take that correlation a step further. Assume that a person is affected by a decreased sense of satisfaction whenever it is cloudy and that it is supposed to rain for a week. How will that affect decision making in the days ahead? Self-awareness of your own triggers and tendencies is valuable in making good decisions and important in regulating a well-lived life.

Life is messy. Few of us get through it without major emotions assailing us…but we don't have to let those emotions continue to threaten us! Be a lion tamer.

Chapter Summary

Life is messy. Few of us get through it without major emotions assailing us, but we don't have to let those emotions derail our decisions or threaten to rip us limb from limb. Be a lion tamer!

- Use the chair and the whip to contain emotions.
- Take the time to process the life experiences that are causing you such an upheaval.
- Put off major life decisions if you can.
- Repeat this process as often as necessary to get those lions under control.

In the next chapter, you will learn how to live without regrets.

17

LIVE WITHOUT REGRETS

"It's an old habit. I spent my life trying not to be careless—
women and children can be careless, but not men."

— The Godfather

Have any of you *not* seen a suspenseful scene in which our hero is running for all he's worth, looking over his shoulder for an evil chasing him from behind? It's too bad that many of us approach life in the same way, only it's a caricature of ourselves chasing another version of ourselves, the stuff of nightmares.

Sometimes preconceived notions of how our life *should* look, what we *should* have accomplished, and what *others* are doing mushrooms into gigantic proportions. Sometimes life's decisions have altered the course of our destiny, and we want to look back, wondering how life might have been different.

These regrets are never helpful. First of all, there is no

way to predict how life would have been better, happier, or more prosperous had we decided one way or the other. Second, in almost every instance, we have learned it is impossible to retrace your steps and obliterate the consequences of your decisions. Without learning how to drop them, we carry those regrets with us through all our lives.

The trick is to turn them into stepping stones rather than millstones. It's an important distinction. A stepping stone is a way to use past experience to our best advantage. A millstone drowns us in a sea of sadness, and some never regain their equilibrium. A stepping stone involves some intentional action.

- 'Fess up. Assuming the responsibility for a mistake isn't easy, and most people prefer blaming others or justifying themselves. I have played that game as well. It's easy and eases my discomfort, but it's counterproductive when it comes to living a life without regrets. Understand that consequences are an eternal principle. Newton's third law states: For every motion, there is an equal and opposite reaction. You are free to make choices in life. However, you are not free from the consequences of your decisions or the actions you take.
- Let that confession work its way through the full range of emotions threatening to overwhelm you. You may be sad. You may be mad at yourself or someone else. You may want to yell a little or shake your fist at heaven. These are all steps in accepting your part in what took place. It's part of owning the situation.
- Take some time to process what you learned.

Life's lessons are not to be squandered on wishing the experience away, but rather, embracing each as a way to live a better life. Lessons are like Tom Hanks in giving Hooch a bath in the classic *Turner and Hooch*. "This is why my kind will dominate the earth..." in describing opposable thumbs. The goal is to distill all that angst and hubris and rage into a statement or short paragraph. When you reach this stage, you have figured out life's lesson.

- Decide what you want to do with it. It may be an experience you'll avoid at all costs. It may be a decision to help another. Transcending regret and taking redemptive action is the ultimate expression of a life well-lived.

Realize that time never erases the memory of your poor decision or dreadful experience. I think that is life's way of putting an exclamation point to a sad chapter, so it doesn't get repeated. But knowing something happened isn't the same thing as *regretting* that it happened. One is a knowledge of the past; the other is a millstone of self-degradation.

At first, a person tries to bandage up the pain of regret. Some leave the bandage on way too long, and the wound gets dirty or infected. Some get so used to the bandage that they never get around to getting rid of it. The idea, though, is to heal. To get past needing a bandage at all. Once you have been through the stages of dealing with regret, it's time for a little self-care. A caveat: don't be premature. This is given *after* you've processed the experience.

Forgive yourself. You knew less back then. You were unprepared. You didn't have the life skills you now process. Life caught you unaware. All of these situations lead us to poor decisions and resultant regret, but very often, in hindsight, we can realize that we only deserve a modicum of the blame. It can be chalked up to the vagaries of life without blaming anyone else or deflecting self-responsibility.

Devise ways to protect yourself from making the same type of mistake in the future. If you have discovered you are prone to making poor decisions when you are angry, employ a self-regulated timeout after an upsetting incident. Many of us are prone to poor decisions when a primal emotion like envy, hurt, or disloyalty descends upon us. In each of those instances, a waiting period before acting is a valuable safeguard.

The other aspect of regret stems from living a life without lofty goals. We've touched on goal setting here and there, but realize that you get from life only what you put into it.

Low expectations = Low results

What characterizes lofty goals? Think of things that almost make you tingle with anticipation or produce a little sweat at the mere audacity that you might be successful. Set goals that make you stretch. Imagine what you might accomplish if the sky was the limit, if no obstacles held you back, and money was never an issue.

These pie-in-the-sky goals may not be realistic, but you can always temper them to make them achievable. It's much harder to take a dumbed-down goal and infuse it with more energy. Try it. Let's consider rearranging furniture in the den to building a rec center for your AV equipment. One is pretty mundane, the other may sound unreachable...but what if you took that lofty aspiration of a whole new entertainment center and tempered it with setting up a wall-hung flat-screen television projector? Don't renovate the room. Don't put in a wet bar. Don't add surround sound. Take just one piece of the dream and make it a reality.

See how the lofty goal becomes more of a reality? Isn't that a lot more satisfying than just rearranging the furniture? Give yourself permission to take any small idea and imagine it into an achievable reality. Don't lower your expectations, and you will never experience the regret of unsatisfying achievement.

In closing this chapter, let's just agree: a life well lived is a life without regret. You hold the key to a better life, and you have the power to unlock the satisfaction of a life well-lived.

Chapter Summary

Learning to turn regret from a millstone into a stepping stone is a life skill you can master. It changes your perspective and prevents you from making the same mistakes over and over again.

- Take responsibility for your decisions.
- Look for what you learned from the experience.
- Learn to impose a self-regulatory timeout when emotions threaten a good decision.

In the next chapter, you will learn why it is so important to insulate yourself from pressure.

18

TAKE A TRIP TO THE BATHROOM

"Until you decide, everything remains possible."

— Mr. Nobody

Sometimes the decisions we face are fraught with pressure. It comes in two ways: one is when you are pressured to make a decision because time or money or the situation is forcing you to come to a conclusion before you are ready. The other way is when your decision is being affected by those around you. Both forms of pressure are insidious and detrimental. Let's begin with situational pressure.

Dr. Danny Friedland, CEO of *Supersmart Health,* uses a sports analogy, saying, "making a tough decision is a game of inches." No matter what your favorite sport may be, we're all aware of what a few inches mean in scoring a goal. His few inches represented the difference between a decision based on thought as opposed to a decision made from another part of the brain a few inches away, based on emotion. A situational pressure increases anxiety and triggers a host of past emotions and remembered experiences, none of which may be helpful in making a reasoned decision.

His advice looks amazingly like our own formula for making a good decision. Figure out the problem. Collect data. Come up with options. Evaluate the best option. Act without regret. No matter what pressure you feel, barring working in an ICU with critically ill patients, there is always a way to work reason into your process. Imagine you're driving down the highway on a road trip with a bunch of friends. At the last stop, someone jumped behind the wheel, and this new driver is weaving all over the road, not paying attention and driving way too fast. It's time to call out, "I have to go to the bathroom."

Yeah, I know. It sounds cheesy, but you'd be amazed how many people, from motorists to CEOs, respect a bathroom break. There is no place more private sometimes than a bathroom stall with the door shut, and those blessed moments of introspection offer you a perfect opportunity to think things through. Admittedly, you don't have all day...but a day is not usually necessary. In fact, some researchers postulate that a decision made under pressure can be the best decision possible if you take just a few moments to think.

Sometimes the pressure we feel comes from the unknown, and the recent pandemic is a case at point. Risk assessment and how to respond to the virus became an issue for everyone on the planet. It required looking at facts as they unfolded. It was a matter of taking time for reflection. Many face the unknown as if it is a time bomb just waiting to explode, but that is not generally the case. More often, taking time to think is always key to good decision making. Think of your tribe. Protecting the most vulnerable is the humane thing to do. Focus on the desired outcome.

These are not rocket science calculations, yet it felt like a majority of the world population was unable to process these basic steps into congruent action. They allowed themselves to be fearful of the unknown and pressured into over- or under-reaction. Think of the hoarding of toilet paper in the United States contrasted with those who insisted there was nothing to it; it was all a hoax. The fear of the unknown can pressure us into unrealistic, untenable decisions...but don't let it. Take that trip to the bathroom and figure it out sanely!

The pressure we feel from others isn't handled by a trip to the bathroom, however. Being part of a family or tribe implies a willingness to follow the tribe's rules or mores. This comes to a head when a decision needs to be made, and the will of the tribe runs counter to the best interests of the will of the individual. A classic example is the book *Lord of the Flies,* in which children are stranded without supervision, and their prior values devolve into mob rule.

The negative impact of peer pressure is an established fact when we talk about impressionable young people without the ego strength to make a personal decision that defies tribal expectations. But let me ask you: Are adults immune from pressure? If you're honest, you'll admit that sadly, we are not. Pressures in adulthood just look different from those experienced in teen-segregated cliques. Adults often feel pressured to fit into office groups, to line up on certain sides in office politics, or to conform to a boss's opinion despite thinking otherwise. Adults also experience pressure within social circles when religion or politics enter the conversation.

Studies done independently by multiple researchers confirm that adolescents and young adults into their mid-twenties are affected by peer pressure. Some never outgrow that weakness. Arrested development or traumatic stress can freeze a person in time, so to speak, and cause the same weaknesses at age 18 to still be prevalent at age 40. As society tends to postpone its coming of age into adulthood, that number may begin to stretch further and further into the personal timeline.

In some ways, I am not sure we ever outgrow that tendency to be affected by pressure. Older adults report they are often pressured by their children to adopt a certain viewpoint or make a particular decision they would shy away from on their own. If we can't avoid pressure and we can't outgrow it, what is the answer? Developing the internal strength, the ego strength to stand on your own despite all pressure may be one of the most valuable and elusive lessons learned in adulthood.

Let's look back at the genesis of peer pressure in adolescence because it has a lot to do with the pressure we succumb to as adults. Pleasurable decisions cause the brain to release a little jolt of dopamine, and many young people make decisions just for that dopamine release. It leads to addiction or other self-destructive behaviors when pleasure cannot be denied in the face of overwhelming personal cognizance that it's a problem. Adults who never learn to rein in those desires for cheap hits of dopamine fall prey to that same result no matter how old they get.

A look at the pattern of decision making in adolescence also reveals the lack of strength to stand up for personal convictions in the face of ridicule or pressure to fit in. Insecure youth may be scarred by these bullying types of situations and enter adulthood, still unwilling to stand up to the bullies of the boardroom or the coffee klatch. Insecure adults surround themselves with buffers and find it easier to go with the flow than make personal decisions. That abdication only postpones the developmental task of learning to stand up for one's self.

The same basic steps of decision making begin this transformative stage of life. Know the problem. Collect data. Come up with options. Assign a value or risk to each option. Choose the best option and move forward. It's after this is done that the difficult work of standing up for your decision comes into play. Here are some ideas to help you:

- Get comfortable in your own shoes. Knowing yourself is a huge step forward.
- Be assertive. This is much more than just stating your preference or decision. It is stating it with conviction. Practice saying it in front of a mirror. Find a pause in the conversation and insert it. Just do it.
- Reward yourself. Yes, you still deserve that dopamine hit but be the person in charge of giving it, not the recipient. You can decide if the reward is a vacation or a chocolate chip cookie, but be reasonable here. It needs to be as immediate as possible and commensurate with the risk you've taken. None of us really need help on this step, because we all know what we'd like deep down inside.

Another way to look at this is to view yourself as a precious work of art. If you had a choice to be adorned with gold or plaster of Paris, which would you choose? We all want to feel our own intrinsic worth, so it behooves us to cultivate the inner strength used to stand up for our own decisions.

Chapter Summary

No one is born with self-assurance. It is cultivated with skill and intentional experience. If you find yourself low, prime the pump. You can grow this commodity and are not bound by past experience.

- When pressured by a situation, take a trip to the bathroom. Take a few moments to consider.
- When you are pressured by others, give yourself permission to state your own preference or decision.
- We never outgrow the need to build on our storehouse of self-assurance. Cultivate a strong sense of self.

In the next chapter, you will learn how to limit the throes of anxiety. Do you know why it's called a silent killer?

19

TAME YOUR ANXIETY

"Anxiety is like a rocking chair. It gives you something to do, but it doesn't get you very far."

— Jodi Picoult

A RECENT STUDY REVEALED THAT INTENSE PRESSURE (ANXIETY) could reduce your cognitive reasoning by up to 25%. That's more than a full grade point average when it comes to test anxiety and a clear example of how destructive anxiety may be in other areas of your life. Think about it. Suppose a "B" is riding on the successful outcome of a final exam. You may not know everything, so let's assume you studied hard and might have earned an "A" with a score of 90%. Now take about 25% because of your anxiety, and you just dropped to 65%, a failing score in many colleges.

Extrapolate that 25% loss of function in all of life, and you may not be living the life you envisioned. It's time to do something about it.

Anxiety causes your brain to form counterproductive

circuitry, and it's hard to break out of it. Endless worry causes you to lose focus and makes it harder to think effectively. It affects your rest with sleeplessness, escalating to nightmares without resolution of the problem. Stress lowers your immune system, making you vulnerable to whatever virus is going around. Soon you feel so overwhelmed that you may be unable to make the correlation between decision paralysis and your current state of health.

Other symptoms of decision anxiety are reflected in skin breakouts, the inability to sit still, fixating on electronics or other pleasures that distract you from your feelings, and a worsening of current mental health issues. For example, a moody person goes into a blue funk. A manic person gets too restless to sit still or sleep. A professional treats the symptoms, but only *you* can treat the cause.

The more common synonym for anxiety is *stress*, and it affects not just your decision making, but your overall health. The father of stress studies was Hans Selye, whose stress research still forms the basis of treatment at the American Institute of Stress. He correlated the relationship of sickness being the outcome of stress. In one study, a controlled group was injected with a virus known to cause the common cold. Not surprisingly, those who had previously reported a stressful experience or who received less sleep or endured other life stresses caught a cold. More interestingly, most of the others did not.

Let's accept that stress is a problem. Let's also accept that stress accompanies most of our decision making. As noted earlier, simple decisions of chocolate or vanilla are often made on a subconscious level, causing no stress at all in the process. The decision to buy a new or used car, however, introduces a lot of uncertainty, unknown variables, and anxiety into the decision-making process. That's stressful, and much of life is dotted with similar stressful decisions.

If thorny issues are to be a regular life occurrence, just how do we diminish the accompanying level of stress? It isn't easy, or you wouldn't be reading this book! Indeed, learning how to dissociate oneself from the stress or angst that goes with decision making is why some get paid big bucks and others only minimum wage. There are some bosses who don't deserve a title or its compensation because they climb upon the backs of those beneath them, but there are countless others who make difficult decisions, and most certainly, those are decisions the rest of us are glad they make, rather than us.

The important point to realize is that stress is stress. Whether you are handling the mind-boggling decisions of a CEO or deciding how to invest your savings, which is a personal nail biter, the effect of the stress is the same. It is unhealthy and possibly debilitating. Further, it precludes making a good decision. Even small amounts of stress caused test respondents to make bad choices, and that includes you. The idea is to lower that stress *before* you make the decision.

Here are some suggestions for handling the anxiety that comes with making big decisions. Some will work better for you than others. Some will work better in some situations than others. Not one of them is perfect for you or for every time you need a way to lower your anxiety level. Rather, get acquainted with the various options and use what you think will work. Try another tactic if your first effort doesn't seem to help. This is a matter of personal thought and personal action.

- Take time out. Didn't we just talk about that? Yup.

Give yourself a trip to the bathroom, and if you can, delay for a day or two before making the commitment.
- Plan some "spa minutes" into each day. Learn how to de-stress each day, so it doesn't accumulate in huge proportions.
- It's okay to solicit feedback from a loosey-goosey friend. Chicken Little would have saved himself a lot of angst if before he decided to run around squawking about the sky falling down, he had consulted someone a little less high-strung than himself.

You can be your own best friend when it comes to handling stress. Develop a positive attitude. Accept that some things just happen and don't allow yourself to get thrown by circumstances. Exercise regularly. Listen to relaxing music. Schedule times for meditation or reflection. Slowing down the pace of life removes a great deal of resident anxiety. Eat a healthy diet. Establish boundaries to keep toxic people out of your life. Think of stress as being a reservoir of anxiety. If you let your reservoir run at maximum capacity, any new stressor will put you over the edge. If you keep your reservoir at low levels, there is less pressure when stress comes your way.

Chapter Summary

Anxiety is a constant in life. You will not be able to prevent it, but you may be able to contain it. The anxiety of making a decision can be crippling, and it's up to you to determine what levels of stress you are willing to consider normal. The lower your stress, the better your health.

- The basics of decision making are still your best friend.
- You can handle the unknowns of life if you face them head-on.
- Stress is a killer, and you are in control of the amount of stress you let into your own life.

In the next chapter, you will learn the problem with marshmallows.

20
MARSHMALLOWS AND INSTANT GRATIFICATION

"Instant gratification is not soon enough."

— MERYL STREEP

HOW MUCH ARE YOU GOVERNED BY INSTANT GRATIFICATION? The answer may surprise you. Those who suffer the yo-yo effects of dieting or who battle any form of substance abuse know it's a problem for them, but instant gratification is a powerful motivator for everyone on the planet. After all, if you won the lottery and had the choice of ten million dollars in a lump sum or spread out in payments over a lifetime, which would you choose? Are you sure of that?

A long-term research project started in the 1960s. Young children were given a plate of goodies, like marshmallows, and told they could eat them immediately, but if they waited, they would receive a second even larger treat. The adult then left the room, leaving the children to stew over whether or not to eat their goodies. Hidden behind mirrored glass, researchers recorded how long the children held out, how many licked their treats, or immediately devoured them. These children were evaluated over time, and it was discovered that holding out on the marshmallow was a predictor of future performance for children of well-educated families.

These children performed better in their studies, scored higher test scores for college, experienced more self-assurance, and performed better in several codices of life (coping skills, substance abuse, etc.). In short, their ability to delay gratification became a pattern of better decision making for years to come. It offers us a glimpse into how we might improve our own life decisions: what is the obvious pleasure? Postpone it. Sometimes that's easier said than done.

What are some of the reasons why we find ourselves unable to delay gratification, even when we know it is in our own best interest to wait? Researchers list ten reasons why people sometimes choose the immediate despite the obvious benefit of delayed gratification.

- Three reasons relate to time itself. We hate delays. We may fear that age will preclude enjoying the object of our desire, or times are too uncertain to be sure we'll get the reward if we wait. In each of these instances, we just can't promise ourselves the wait will be worth it.
- Two reasons result from our lack of knowledge. We either cannot imagine the value of waiting or can't figure out how it might influence a better outcome.
- One reason is very powerful. Poverty influences our ability to wait on outcomes because the immediate need is so pressing.
- Three reasons were completely outside the realm of reason. Impulse control, mood, and an

inability to govern emotions all lowered will power or the ability to delay gratification.
- The last was anticipation. Sometimes there just isn't enough resident willpower to wait.

Take a moment and think about the last time you looked at an upcoming event or piece of pie or some other temptation which you thought you ought to reject...but didn't. Now figure out which of these reasons applied to your lack of willpower.

The antidote to these problems is amazingly easy to employ. Get more sleep. Exercise. Look at the decision from a larger perspective. Know your own weaknesses and fortify yourself when temptation darkens your path. Devote some time each day to self-care. These aren't hard to do, but it can be hard to *make yourself do them*. Perhaps willpower is a little more elusive, and they are longer-term alternatives.

Measure your progress. If immediate gratification is an issue for you when it comes to sweets, tracking that number on the scale is a way to keep track of your weight and be proud of your accomplishment. If money burns a hole in your pocket the week you get paid, keep track of your expenditure and the reserve you have left at the end of the paycheck to track your progress and be pleased with your growing self-control.

Set priorities. Deciding on what is most important can help you delay gratifying that twinge most resistant to control. If sweets are your Achilles heel, keep your eye on that new dress you want to get into. If controlling your paycheck is the issue, tape a picture of that big-ticket item you're salivating over onto your mirror. Make lists. Keep track of what is important.

Take a deep breath. Sometimes what we need most in

delaying gratification is just a deep breath to keep us grounded. Any action that allows you time to regather your defenses works, but a deep breath is cleansing and symbolic of a fresh start.

Banish Temptation. This is a bit of a crutch to some people, but just remove the source of your delight. Don't allow sweets into the house. Put your money into the bank straightway, and stop carrying around a charge card.

Change the wording. Turn the self-defeat of "I can't" into the action of "I don't." There is a world of difference between believing you cannot wait for something you want and deliberately thinking, "I don't want to get this now" or "I don't want to disappoint myself" or "I don't choose to wait." The last choice is still immediate gratification, but it at least is a choice to give in, as opposed to believing you had no choice in the matter. An action statement is more likely to foster the inner strength to resist temptation than a defeatist attitude.

Devise a plan. If you have a plan on how you are going to achieve your goal, you are more likely to stick to the plan than find yourself resorting to immediate gratification. If sweets are a problem for you, have a plan for incorporating a more healthy alternative into your diet. Not perfect, but better. If retail therapy is your issue, budget the time and amount you allow yourself to spend. The plan will not always work, but it's a definite step in the right direction.

This is imperative if you have a weakness in impulse control and have children of your own. Those little eyes are watching you, and very likely there is some remediation you need to do for them as well. Letting a child grow up caught in the web of immediate gratification poses significant problems. These children will take for granted whatever you can afford to give them and still be dissatisfied. They will have no patience and a close to zero tolerance level for frustration. These qualities may not be overwhelming at the age of four, but think of having to deal with these same behaviors at fourteen, magnified and ingrained, hard to reverse. Many of these children end up with substance abuse problems or find themselves in correctional facilities when they cannot control their impulses.

It begins with getting yourself under control and then taking your child's behavior in hand, setting limits. Expect some resistance, but be tougher and more persistent than your child. Begin by rewarding patient behavior. Model self-control. Help them visualize the rewards of waiting for what they want, for perhaps earning what they want. Teach them strategies for developing patience: mark a date on the calendar and cross off intervening days, count backward, do something else. Distractions are a big help. Help them complete "if, then" statements. *If I clean the bathroom, then I can play in the pool.* As you teach them, you will be reinforcing this strength in yourself. You can do this!

The important point in this chapter is to control the way you award yourself pleasure. Stop living for the moment and learn to live for the next day or month or year from now. Delayed gratification is a great way to hold off those spur-of-the-moment decisions so many of us come to lament later.

Chapter Summary

Delayed gratification is an important part of decision making because it takes you from a poor decision to a better one. The first thought that comes to your mind in guessing may work for you, but natural proclivities are no way to govern your life decisions.

- Figure out why delayed gratification is an issue for you.
- Look at the strategies for conquering this tendency to decide on what you want the moment you want it. Decide on one.
- Practice self-control by trying various other coping mechanisms, and find what works best for you. Being committed to the best is better than being okay. It's okay to like marshmallows, but waiting for a better treat just makes good sense.

In the next chapter, you will learn the lesson of the Cheshire Cat.

21

ALICE LEARNED THE HARD WAY

"The path of least resistance is the path of the loser."

— H.G. Wells

When I was first introduced to Alice and her adventures through the looking glass, I was horrified. First of all, I didn't like the idea of growing larger or smaller based on what you ate or drank, because even at that age, I knew you don't eat anything your mom hasn't given you. Then I hated the way she meandered through all those horrid experiences. It was my first taste of angst in watching the choices of someone outside of myself, and it never grew more enjoyable. The Cheshire cat said it well when asked which path to take, "If you don't know where you want to go, it doesn't matter which path you take." *The path of least resistance leads nowhere.*

Years later, I watched *Gone with the Wind* and grew just as impatient with Scarlett O'Hara. I wanted to reach into the screen and just slap her silly! Could she never make a good decision? By that stage in life, I knew this maxim to be true: *The path of least resistance leads nowhere.* Phrased another way and more positively, "Live for today with a plan for tomorrow." Obviously, some decisions are imperative for day-to-day survival, but stopping there is tantamount to following the path of least resistance.

A successful life, looked back upon in later years, shows the path of a person who had a goal, who changed the goal along the way or zig-zagged a little here or there, but had a goal in mind. A life of purpose, one guided by an overarching goal, is the opposite of the path of least resistance.

Life follows the path of least resistance. Gravity, the flow of water, even Google maps, will direct you in the fastest and most direct route. Shouldn't we? Not necessarily. Researchers tested this hypothesis by asking students to respond to moving clouds of dots. They were asked to move the joystick right if the cloud was moving right and left if the cloud was moving left. That's pretty straightforward, isn't it? The experiment didn't end there. They programmed the joystick to add *resistance to the direction the dots were moving.* For example, if the dots moved right, suddenly the joystick required effort to move it to the right. If the cloud moved to the left, the joystick suddenly was harder to move to the left. The outcome may surprise you.

The students moved the joystick in the direction of least resistance and convinced themselves that *that was the direction the dots were moving.* There's a term for this: *cognitive dissonance.* It's when your eyes say one thing, but your brain says something else. The two don't match up. The natural instinct is to accept the lie.

Think about one of Aesop's fables, the one where the fox spies some perfectly ripe, plump juicy grapes high overhead. After trying multiple times to reach them, he switches to the low lying fruit with the rationalization, "Those grapes up there were probably sour, anyway." The fox takes the path of least resistance. The fox convinces himself it's the right thing to do. Hmm.

What implications does that have for you? Think about current trends. Your parents and grandparents found a good company, started at the bottom and worked their way up the ladder, retiring from the company with a decent pension. What's the current trend? Fewer companies offer pensions, older workers get canned in favor of inexpensive new hires, and workers are constantly looking for that better job with no company loyalty. The shift from loyalty and mutual benefit to greed and self-interest has produced an unstable job market with workers following the path of least resistance.

Got a petty grievance? Split and get another job. *See a job that nets a dollar more per hour?* Split and get another job. What happens, though, when we follow this attractive path of least resistance?

- Arrested social growth. We all enter adulthood with a few rough edges. Those used to get rubbed off by co-workers and bosses who would rather have us on time than late, or amenable to taking assignments rather than thinking we know it all. When we are easily aggrieved at constructive criticism and just split, those rough edges go with us. We fail to learn how to fit in, be productive, and work as part of the team. The workforce never grows up. It just gets more and more self indulgent.
- Arrested self-growth. Maslow's stages of development suggest that individuals who live

> fulfilled lives never stop growing, never stop developing into a richer version of themselves. When we fail to accept life's lessons, we stop growing. Selfish young adults become selfish older adults. The fabric of society weakens because its members never mature fully.

The path of least resistance is not the path of growth and personal fulfillment. It's just the path to easy work, easy money, and disposable personal relationships. Yes, I am advocating the harder path. It means doing the right thing, the moral thing. It involves some perseverance and takes some fortitude when it proves more challenging than once imagined.

Lee Ann Womack sang, "I hope you never fear those mountains in the distance. Never settle for the path of least resistance." Her transcendental message is clear. If you want to dance, you have to strive for the experience that *transcends* the ordinary. One of my favorite quotes is "Reach for the moon. If you miss it, you'll land among the stars." I want to encourage you to live up to the high calling of doing your best, always becoming your best. When you reach that juncture of least resistance, ask yourself what the reward is to persevere. Encourage yourself to compete, not retreat. Ask yourself if you're willing to pay the cost of quitting.

Implicit in the concept of following the path of least resistance is the hidden agreement with the universe that you will *settle* for something less than ideal. What happens when you begin down that slippery slope? Taking the easy way out means that you miss the vista of achievement. That view of the world at your feet just never happens if you turn away from the summit when the trail grows steep. Settling is another name for defeat.

. . .

Henry David Thoreau is credited with penning, "the path of least resistance leads to crooked roads and crooked men." Jails are full of people taking shortcuts to get what they wanted, following the path of least resistance. The ultimate end of the path of least resistance is not where you want to land.

How do you avoid the path of least resistance? Decide on where you are going. Set goals. Plot a course. Deliberately set your sights on an accomplishment and persevere. It's a decision. It is intentional forward progress despite all obstacles. Bear in mind a few key principles:

- **The path offers as much joy as the vista.** Researchers have concluded that setting loftier goals increases personal happiness. Each step forward is an accomplishment the path of least resistance never offers.
- **Focus on the journey.** Researchers have also concluded that in setting goals to perform better, participants enjoyed greater self-satisfaction along the way than those who focused only on reaching the outcome. So expect the hike uphill to be as fulfilling as the summit itself. Good to know!
- **Focus on being a better you.** The third conclusion of researchers is that goals focused on self-improvement offered more satisfaction than goals for external pleasures. For example, becoming a better facilitator offered more self-satisfaction than the raise for being a better facilitator. The pleasure came with

achievement, not the evidence of the achievement.

Very truly, the path of least resistance leads nowhere. Alice wandered through the Looking Glass and found no direct path back home. Let's not follow *her* example!

Chapter Summary

Taking the high road is the very opposite of taking the path of least resistance. Yet it's that high road that leads to panoramic vistas and the sweet joy of accomplishment. I want to encourage you to resist the reduced expectations so prevalent in society today. Decide to live a life of being your best self. It's well worth it!

- The road less traveled will offer you more personal growth and self-satisfaction.
- The road less traveled improves the fabric of society.
- Set goals. Lofty goals.
- Focus on the path and on being a better you for the most joy in the trek to the summit.

In the next chapter, you will learn how to navigate those murky waters of complex decisions.

22

BREW A BETTER CUP OF TEA

"I must have a prodigious amount of mind; it takes me as much as a week, sometimes, to make it up!"

— MARK TWAIN

BY NOW, YOU KNOW THAT I LIKE TO WORK MY WAY INTO OUR material with an example and a way to relate to it in practical ways. That's why I looked at my morning routine as a way to resolve life's thorniest decisions. Begin with the first light of day and apply the test of tea.

I like to brew a cup of tea in the morning. Now, I'm not a teabag kind of person. Uh uh. I learned early on that a good cup of tea comes with several requirements:

1. Begin with a good tea.
2. The pot is important.
3. Don't boil the water.
4. Let the tea steep in the pot.
5. Remove the tea leaves before the pot turns bitter.

I know, who knew it was such a complex process? The Chinese have been fine-tuning the tea ceremony for centuries, but I'm more into the British idea of a cup of good tea without any mystical trappings. I admit to being a tea snob, and I love to get my tea from Murchie's, paying exorbitant shipping from a commonwealth country. A ceramic pot is important, and its spout must be curved to pour the tea without a mess. The water must be at the boiling temperature but not whistling in the teapot. I let my tea steep for three to five minutes before lifting the leaves from the pot. If I leave it too long, it becomes bitter, and I have to water it down to make it palatable.

You may be wondering what any of this has to do with making a complex decision. I think you'll find in retrospect that it has *everything* to do with the process of brewing a good cup of tea. Let's begin with some basic premises.

Life is full of hard, complex decisions. We've brushed against them several times: choice of a life companion, choosing a career, accepting a job, buying a home...these are all complex decisions. They're hard because they are riddled with multiple factors and because their outcomes are masked. There's no way to accurately predict the outcome of a choice one way or the other. So how do we make these complex decisions?

Post your goals in front of you. It is never more important in knowing your goals as when you face an important, life-changing complex decision. Do this before you list any options or look at any possibilities to avoid bias. Your brain can trick you into accepting the first thing it sees, but that first thing needs to meet your expectations.

Think about car hunting. One primal hunter lists every desirable option. The hunter researches all known makes and models to assess each option. That same intrepid hunter searches all the lots within a hundred miles to find the *best* option. I know this is true because I am married to an intrepid hunter.

The happy hunter knows exactly what brings joy. This hunter realizes that every hunting ground has the same kinds of wildlife, so why visit all of them? The happy hunter goes to a lot, finds the best choice available, and makes a final decision on what brings joy. Done. I know this because I am a happy hunter.

Primal hunters and happy hunters often live in the same ecosystem and must learn that each has merit. The common denominator in this equation of differences is their combined set of goals. If each is basing a decision on the same set of goals, it can be a harmonious decision despite their differing methodology. The same set of goals will produce similar outcomes. Just don't try to hunt together.

Reduce the equation. Remember fractions? The bane of my existence? One thing I did learn pretty early on is the value of reducing an equation *before* solving the problem. It was easier to deal with smaller numbers and coefficients than larger ones. That holds true in life as well.

Break down the big decisions into all the little factors affecting the outcome. Buying a home includes factors like how much money you have saved, how much money you are willing to borrow, where you want to live, relative property values, how well a piece of property will weather over time, and the satisfaction in living in a particular neighborhood. None of these are necessarily easy decisions but added together, it's the stuff of nightmares.

If you are a computer buff, think of it this way. Your brain has an unlimited amount of RAM, but a rather limited amount of ROM. The average brain can process seven +/- two variables before steam starts to come out of one's ears. I know we have amazing potential, but that's in our capacity to *remember* things. Our ability to analyze and keep track of variables is limited, so work with your brain, not against it. Reduce all those factors into a graph or spreadsheet and analyze them individually, one at a time.

An important part of this phase of problem-solving is realizing that your brain may need additional information. It's okay to solicit advice about *which factors to analyze*, but not *what decision to make*. Inherent in a good decision is the analysis of all the important factors. Missing one can lead to disaster. Good counsel is always a welcome addition.

What happens when you fail to reduce the variables into manageable bytes of information? If you're like me, a lot of thinking in circles, a decision that just feels wrong, or missing an important piece of information. I simply cannot make a complex decision without a pen and a piece of paper, and usually a notebook. As a writer, I process all of these variables and the multitude of individual smaller decisions with pages of writing to organize my thoughts and keep track of them. Whether you write, draw grids, or make diagrams is irrelevant. Find a way to break down a big decision into all its smaller components.

Realize that your brain really wants to help you. Researchers at MIT discovered that in these multi-factored complex decisions, the brain invokes its own hierarchy in assessing the relevance of each little decision along the way. Given a complex issue, the brain processed multiple actions and assessed its level of confidence in each. Why didn't my brain tell me? Probably because I'm an overthinker and didn't listen!

Take advantage of your brain's ability to analyze and trust that your best decisions are not based on the values of any two choices, but on the *difference between those two values*. For example, choosing whether to attend college or not isn't based on the value of a college education or the value of working with your hands in building houses, but on the differences between those two values: potential income, fulfillment derived, time spent in preparation, and cost of preparation. It's the difference in the number or value in each part of the analysis that determines an eventual decision.

Let's look at one example: the choice of becoming a doctor or working on a road crew. At first look, it seems like the potential for income swings toward professionalism but think again. On the one hand, calculate the earnings of working on a road crew for twelve years. On the other hand, add up the cost of education, the cost of setting up a practice, and the interest on educational loans. A doctor might have to work fifteen years to equal the same income received by the laborer on a road crew. Fulfillment becomes the deciding factor for many interns and residents. Looking at individual factors helps you feel confident about your choice in making a difficult decision.

Don't be afraid to do this logically. List your options, then analyze possible factors. Let's look at buying a house. That's a big decision. Draw yourself a grid with two or three options across the top and two or three lines for options to consider. An obvious item to consider is the cost of the house. Underneath that ask and answer a couple of other questions: What is the expected resale value of the house in five years in a good market? What is the baseline of retail value in a worst-case scenario? An empty lot behind the house may feel appealing right now, but if it houses a convenience store five years from now, how will that affect the property value? Writing down the figures in this exercise helps you visualize not just what you're seeing, but what you may *not* be seeing, and it helps you make a better decision.

Another way to help you decide on the resale value of a particular home would be a comparison of tabulated data. You can build a table listing five neighboring homes and easily determine the sale values to assess a trend. Look at increasing taxed values to determine a pattern. That table suddenly makes it very clear: a home or neighborhood is increasing in value, or it's not. Comparing two sets of data tells you very quickly which home is empirically increasing in value over the other.

When it comes to listing and assessing the factors or underlying decisions, keep a red pencil handy. Don't be afraid to draw a line through the items that sounded significant, but upon reflection, really don't. Let's talk about choosing a college. Three factors may influence your decision: Cost, academics (majors available and earned respect), and social activities. You may contemplate this and realize that the social activities are unimportant to you. You can have a good time wherever you go, and activity fees are highly overrated. Scratch that out. Your decision just got easier, didn't it?

Don't be afraid to draw a picture. Numbers are good for analyzing empirical data, but a picture may be worth a thousand words, isn't that how the saying goes? Sometimes a difficult decision becomes easier when you translate those numbers into a bar graph or pie chart. The visual imagery means more than intangible dollars or hours or figures.

Visual people who love color will appreciate mapping

out the options. Create a chart with options across the top and all the variables down the left side. Assign a color to the most important variable, and so on. Now color in those boxes. A logical decision pops out at you.

Realize that complex decisions often affect others around you. Determine if any or all of those people in your tribe deserve a voice in making the decision. If yes, let each offer an opinion, not a vote. This is not a stockholder's meeting. This is your life. You and you alone make and live with the decision. We covered taking responsibility for your decisions in Chapter Seven.

That does not relieve you of the responsibility of doing what is best for all, however. Self-interest must be tempered with a concern for the most vulnerable, the most dependent, the most needy. Each of those additional need sets become variables, and as before, weigh out the values inherent within each variable, then determine the difference between the values. We began talking about individual responsibility in Chapter Seven, and it's been a theme resonating all the way through this book.

When you accept the responsibility for making a complex decision, you grow in stature. One of my favorite Wild West heroes was John Wayne, known for portraying iconic characters who made tough decisions and stood behind them. When I went back to review his long list of accomplishments, I could find no evidence that he ever accepted a script in which he played an unrepentant outlaw. He chose to focus on modeling moral behavior and left a legacy, not a list of accomplishments.

Accept risk as being inherent in complex decisions. Harry Truman used to say, "No easy decisions come to the desk of the President." He also said, "The buck stops here," implying his willingness to incur the fallout of his decisions. Risk analysis is a fancy way of saying, "Look both ways before crossing the street." It isn't crazy insane. It's common sense. Consequences are a part of every decision, and learning to recognize and weigh them is part of solving complex decisions. Write down a decision looming before you. Now draw a line vertically down the paper under the statement and list the pluses and minuses of moving one direction or the other on each side of the paper.

If you are an overthinker, you'll appreciate this exercise. This is that moment, and the stage is yours. Employ a complicated strategy like a *Futures Wheel* and analyze to your heart's content. Simply draw a circle around one option, Draw arrows radiating outward from this first circle, and list possible outcomes with other arrows and so on. There are always first-order consequences, second or third, or fourth-order consequences. The further your consequences are from the initial statement, the less vital some of those consequences may be. It's all a part of personal risk assessment. Even if you are not an overthinker, this can be a helpful exercise. The easily distracted may find it helpful to capture errant thoughts on paper in a diagram, offering focus as the reward of completing the exercise.

Realize that risk helps you be sure you've uncovered all the options available. Sometimes a complex decision will come your way, and the answer will be *none of the above*. Allow yourself the opportunity to go back and start over when this happens. A big, complicated, and messy life decision only gets messier when you make the wrong choice. Think of the disastrous effects of a failed marriage. It not only leaves scars on the couple itself, but the children suffer as well. Eighteen years of child support can be quite a price to pay for making a bad decision. A lifetime of negative emotions hurts everyone surrounding the failed union.

Accept that there is risk and if the risk is too high, step back. Think again. If you can't accept the level of risk a decision engenders, you may be starting off with the wrong variables...or in this case, the wrong person in mind.

So let's see what tea had to do with any of this.

1. Remember our paradigm for decision making? It always begins by stating or understanding the issue. This is like choosing a good blend of tea. I love #10 blend, made for the Queen Mother herself! When it comes to life's toughest decisions, I like to be sure I have the issue well stated and broken down into all its components. This exercise is the selection of the tea you want to brew. Remember that this is a matter of choice, a gut decision. Never ignore what you know you like in favor of something that sounds good, but you know you don't like it. That's never the right decision.
2. Choose a good pot. Some methodology is involved in resolving a complex decision, and you'll find tools in Chapter 22. When in doubt, always return to our basic paradigm: state the problem, collect data, look at all the options, select an option, assess its value, decide, and move forward. You can't beat that course of action. You may find it laborious to go through all the smaller decisions embedded in a complex issue, but it's a definite option.
3. Don't subject yourself to the boiling temperatures of indecision, pressure, or anxiety.

Be timely. Review those chapters if you're feeling pulled, but realize that your best decision will come when you are at your personal best.
4. Give yourself the gift of time. Let the problem steep in your mind. You can set a deadline (or another may set it for you), but don't even try to make this a spur of the moment resolution.
5. Decide before the issue leaves an unpleasant taste in your mouth, metaphorically speaking. You know what I mean here; don't dwell on this until you and everyone around you is sick of the whole thing.

Making sense of a complex decision is a skill you can learn. Once you've mastered the successful resolution of your first thorny issue, the process will feel less mystical, and you'll feel more secure with your next complex decision.

Chapter Summary

A complex decision is often multiple little decisions, each one having an impact on one large choice staring you in the face. Complex decisions rarely defy analysis, are easy to put to paper, and much less intimidating when you apply some common sense.

- Always, always, know the issue at hand. Know it frontward and backward.
- Break a complex decision into all its parts and factors.
- Draw charts or pictures to visualize what you figure out...a decision may leap off the page!

- Think of others who are impacted by this decision.
- Look at the risk factor. Risk can be exhilarating, but when the stakes are too high, it's time to reconsider.

In the next chapter, you will learn some tools which may help you along the way.

23

TOOLS IN YOUR REPERTOIRE

> *"When you have a few cake formulas and filling ideas in your repertoire, you'll find that it's pretty much an assembly job—you can mix and match every time."*
>
> — JULIA CHILD

BY NOW, YOU HAVE BEEN THROUGH A NUMBER OF EXERCISES. Let's review them and make them easy to apply over and over again. Make copies of these final pages and use them as a workbook when you need help in making decisions. Remember how I said I'd be with you the whole way? This is how my words can assist you long after you've read the book. The process works...just do it!

Determine Your Code of Conduct. List ten values you hold dear and consider the core of your belief system.

1.
2.
3.
4.

5.
6.
7.
8.
9.
10.

Remember that these items can shift up or down in importance, be rewritten, added to, or eliminated. This is *your* belief system. Making a decision you will feel proud of is based on not violating any one of these principles.

A Risk/Probability Chart. You can be scientific in analyzing the risk factors in any decision by devising a chart. Think back to your days in basic geometry. Draw a square. On the left side, write down the probability of any given outcome. Your scale goes from low to high. On the bottom of the chart, write down the impact of that choice. Again, the corner represents a low impact, growing to a high impact. The values you plot inside this square are subjective evaluations of how you imagine the probability and impact of any given choice.

For example, consider exposure to measles. You have planned a family reunion but have just learned one family is recovering from a bout of measles. Should you go or stay at home? Within your chart may be a number of variables. Can you go and enforce social distancing, and if so, what would be the probability of infection and the impact? If your children have been vaccinated and you consider them immune, where will your dot be in the chart? If your children have not been vaccinated and you want them exposed now rather than later, where will you place your dot? As you compare these different values, it is easier to analyze the various options to make a better decision.

Deciding between two good options. Ask yourself some quick questions:

- Can I afford this?
- Can I return this?
- Do I need this?
- Do I have a place to put this?
- Does one set of preferences outweigh the other?
- Will I value this a month from now?
- Do I have anything similar at home already?

These questions make a difference for all those spontaneous choices you make every day. *A choice needs to garner at least three yeses to make it into the acceptable side of the equation.*

The decision-making paradigm.

1. Write down the decision.
2. Compile the data.
3. Figure out the possible outcomes of this decision.
4. Assign each possible outcome a probability score.
5. Obtain feedback.
6. Decide.

Manage Your Regrets.

1. 'Fess up.
2. Let that confession work its way through the full range of emotions threatening to overwhelm you.
3. Take some time to process what you learned.
4. Decide what you want to do with it.

Ward Off Instant Gratification.

1. Set priorities.
2. Take a deep breath.
3. Banish temptation.
4. Change the wording.
5. Devise a plan.

Marginal Analysis. CEOs and statisticians do this...why shouldn't you? On each side of that top line, put a variable. Now add up the minuses of each option. Logically, one option is better than the other.

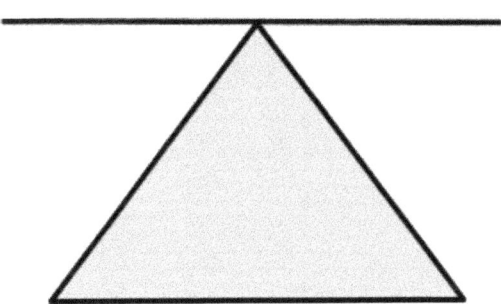

The Pareto Principle. This was initially a business tool but is still an application that can affect your personal decisions. It helps you see what might not normally surface into your sphere of consciousness. The idea is simple: 20% of any factor often adds up to 80% of what you value. When you can identify that factor, decision making is a breeze.

For example, let's say you must decide between two college majors—accounting and business management. You're pretty good at math, and many accountants transition into higher-paying jobs as actuaries. In contrast, many business managers languish on the sales floor or hit a glass ceiling, so it sounds like one might be a better option than the other.

Look at where your satisfaction comes from. How do you spend your time? If your free time is limited and you live for weekends and parties, that 20% of your time yields 80% of your pleasure in life. You're a people person more than a number cruncher. If you're looking for a career that will offer you the most meaning in life, go with a business major.

See how that works? It may seem like a simplistic example, but the numbers are amazingly consistent in other applications.

Build a table. Many complex decisions are made easier when you can objectify the pluses and minuses. Use a table like this to list the options on one side, and the relative costs or values of each from the top down. Color the pluses green and the minuses red for a graphic way to assess the pros and cons of any decision.

OPTIONS	+ OR -	+ OR -	+ OR -	+ OR -

Slice the pie. Another way to visualize all the facets of a decision is to create a pie chart for every option. You can add lines for all the options, and you can adjust those lines to objectify the amount of weight each carries. This example shows how to choose the best team if you are looking at being recruited for college football.

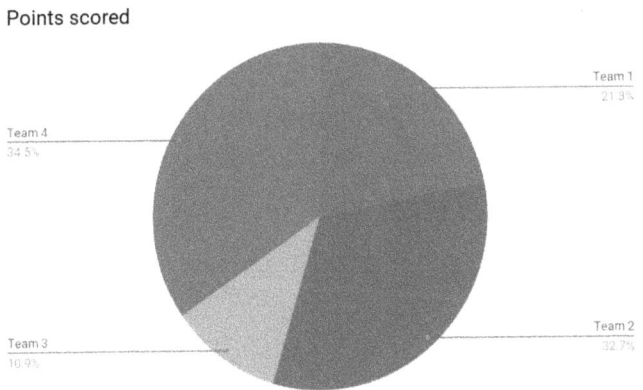

This example shows how to choose the best team if you are looking at being recruited for college football, but a simple circle will help you in most of life's decisions:

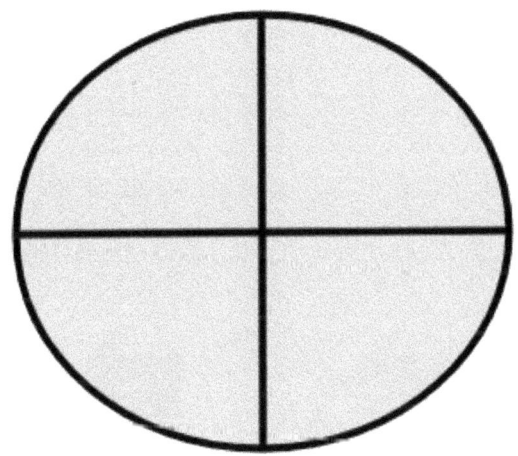

Visit with an empty chair. Sometimes we just don't have the time to visit with a friend or a friend isn't available. A handy trick I've had employed is the empty chair. Sit down and get comfortable. Make sure there's a chair next to you or opposite from you. Imagine your friend or mentor in that chair.

Now think about the thorny decision and all the factors involved. Draw a callout and write down what you think the person in the chair might say.

It's usually good advice, so give it some thought, hint, hint.

Draw an Ishikawa diagram. This is a great way to analyze how you got to a particular place from which you'd like to extricate yourself. Remember, I told you that sometimes options just don't work out. Being able to back up is tricky, especially if you've been on this path awhile and don't remember just how you got to your current place of discomfort.

Put your current status in the third circle, and work your way backward. If you can visualize how you got there, you can figure out how to retrace your steps.

Do a break-even analysis. Often our most worrying decisions involve money. You have an opportunity to get an RV and could travel without paying for hotel rooms. On the surface, it sounds like a great idea, so why not? Call some hotels and figure out the average cost of a night, and divide the amount into the cost of the RV. How many hotel stays would be required for you to break even on the cost of that RV? Now, you may want to factor the ease of packing and the pleasure of having one and the availability of lodging where there may be very few hotels to choose from, so you might decide to go ahead and make the purchase, but be clear and congruent in your decision making.

FINAL WORDS

Let me ask you a question: *How long did it take you to read this book?* Let's say you spent a week reading and digesting the material, working some of the exercises. Do you feel like you're better at making decisions and evaluating all those what-ifs than you were two weeks ago?

Most of us need to build new habits into our lifestyles, and that takes time. I want to encourage you to go through the book a second time. Establish some spending habits. Get used to using the paradigm for decision making on a daily basis. You see, time has to equal a percentage of time.

What does that mean? If you spent 25 years becoming an indecisive person, always second-guessing yourself, two weeks might not be enough time to change and become a whole new person. You have to undo before you can begin the creative work of rebuilding good habits. The act of habit demolition begins when you see an aspect of yourself and mentally cringe. *I want to change that*! Look at your patterns of behavior and your responses to those situations. These help you identify areas of indecision. It takes a little time to get used to the idea, to figure out why you ended up like this, and to figure out what actions make you look indecisive. *Then* comes the work of reconstruction! How much time are we looking at? Not years, but truly ninety+ days.

The reconstruction is the fun part! Remove stumbling blocks. Add new behaviors. Adopt a new look for the new you, some talisman that reminds you: *I'm different now. I'm decisive. I make my own way in the world.* Expect this to take some time and some practice, but your persistence is the key to becoming a decisive person.

I want to encourage you to make a resolution in a very graphic way. Make a motivation board, and place it in a private but prominent place. Think about the things you want in life, and find pictures or graphics for each. Put them on your board, and seeing them reminds you: *Oh yeah, I'm going to...* That decision results in a form of self-actualization, and it begins with your decision to change and your commitment to seeing it through.

Continue your journal entries, because processing those rainy days when your resolve falters or you abdicate your power to decide to someone else helps you enjoy more autonomy. If you grew up a people pleaser, it can be terrifying to assume responsibilities for your own decisions, and standing up for them is especially difficult. Some days you'll slide back into the path of least resistance, just get along, do what someone else wants you to do...but have a conversation with yourself afterward. Why were you feeling low? What situation or phrase or inference made you feel insecure? What might you have done differently? These personal conversations are very, very valuable.

Make multiple copies of your toolkit and keep them in a little notebook. Use them. As you do, you'll find that decision making is not as scary or difficult as you once imagined. Actually, you *are* a decision-making marvel, and you just didn't know it!

BIBLIOGRAPHY

"3 Ways Anxiety Can Affect Decision Making (and What to Do)." *Psychology Today*, https://www.psychologytoday.com/blog/in-practice/201906/3-ways-anxiety-can-affect-decision-making-and-what-do. [Accessed 13 June 2020].

5 Whys: Getting to the Root of a Problem Quickly. http://www.mindtools.com/pages/article/newTMC_5W.htm. [Accessed 13 June 2020].

"10 Reasons We Rush for Immediate Gratification." *Psychology Today*, https://www.psychologytoday.com/blog/science-choice/201606/10-reasons-we-rush-immediate-gratification. [Accessed 17 June 2020].

"12 Reasons You Should Never Regret Any Decision You Ever Make." *Lifehack*, 6 Mar. 2014, https://www.lifehack.org/articles/communication/12-reasons-you-should-never-regret-any-decision-you-ever-make.html.

Authority, University of Wisconsin Hospitals and Clinics. "Dealing with Peer Pressure When You're an Adult." *UW Health*, https://www.uwhealth.org/news/dealing-with-peer-pressure-when-youre-an-adult/46604. [Accessed 17 June 2020].

Berglund, Christopher., 2015. Psychology Today. 2015. *The Neuroscience of Making a Decision.* [online]. Available at: <https://www.psychologytoday.com/us/blog/the-athletes-way/201505/the-neuroscience-making-decision> [Accessed 11 June 2020].

Boyd, Danielle. "Hans Selye: Birth of Stress." *The American Institute of Stress*, https://www.stress.org/about/hans-selye-birth-of-stress. [Accessed 17 June 2020].

"Brain: How to Optimize Decision Making?" *ScienceDaily*, https://www.sciencedaily.com/releases/2019/09/190911101537.htm. [Accessed 13 June 2020].

Bridges, Frances. "5 Ways To Improve Self-Control." *Forbes*, https://www.forbes.com/sites/francesbridges/2018/06/28/5-ways-to-improve-self-control/. [Accessed 17 June 2020].

BuzzFeed. 2020. *27 Everyday Decisions That Twentysomethings Are Really Bad At Making.* [online] Available at: <https://www.buzzfeed.com/regajha/everyday-decisions-that-twenty-somethings-are-really-bad> [Accessed 8 June 2020].

Clark, Jeremy J., et al. "Pavlovian Valuation Systems in Learning and Decision Making." Current Opinion in Neurobiology, vol. 22, no. 6, Dec. 2012, pp. 1054–61. PubMed Central, doi:10.1016/j.conb.2012.06.004.

Cohen, Sheldon, et al. "Ten Surprising Facts About Stressful Life Events and Disease Risk." *Annual Review of Psychology*, vol. 70, Jan. 2019, pp. 577–97. *PubMed Central*, doi:10.1146/annurev-psych-010418-102857.

Decision-Making and the Brain. https://neuro.hms.harvard.edu/harvard-mahoney-neuroscience-institute/brain-newsletter/and-brain/decision-making-and-brain. [Accessed 13 June 2020].

Demetri, Daniel. "5 Essential Tools for Conquering Complex Decisions." *Medium*, 22 Aug. 2016, https://medium.com/earnest-product-management/5-essential-tools-for-conquering-complex-decisions-8dd2d2279458.

Facebook, et al. "The Surprising Thing the 'marshmallow Test' Reveals about Kids in an Instant-Gratification World." *Los Angeles Times*, 26 June 2018, https://www.latimes.com/science/sciencenow/la-sci-sn-marshmallow-test-kids-20180626-story.html

Fuhrmann, Cynthia N., et al. "Narrowing the Choices: What Career Path Is Right for You?" *Science | AAAS*, 23 Sept. 2013, https://www.sciencemag.org/careers/2013/09/narrowing-choices-what-career-path-right-you. [Accessed 13 June 2020].

Goodman, N., 2020. *5 Ways To Learn To Trust Your Instincts*. [online] Entrepreneur. Available at: <https://www.entrepreneur.com/article/225304> [Accessed 8 June 2020].

"How People Make Decisions." *Smashing Magazine*, 7 Feb. 2019, https://www.smashingmagazine.com/2019/02/human-decision-making/.

"How We Make Complex Decisions." *MIT News*, http://news.mit.edu/2019/how-brain-complex-decisions-0516. [Accessed 18 June 2020].

Huffpost.com. 2020. *Huffpost Is Now A Part Of Verizon Media*. [online] Available at: <https://www.huffpost.com/entry/the-8020-view-of-choices_b_5524883> [Accessed 8 June 2020].

Inc.com. 2020. *20 Ways To Attract Good Luck*. [online] Available at: <https://www.inc.com/christina-desmarais/20-ways-to-attract-good-luck.html> [Accessed 6 June 2020].

Keys To Making a Good Decision. https://www.essential-lifeskills.net/gooddecision.html. [Accessed 13 June 2020].

Lamia, Mary. "Your Gut Is Smarter than You Think — and It Can Help You Make Better Decisions, According to a Psychologist." *Business Insider*, https://www.businessinsider.com/decisions-gut-instincts-psychologist-2018-7. Accessed 18 June 2020

"Letting Go of Regrets." *Psychology Today*, https://www.psychologytoday.com/blog/understand-other-people/201704/letting-go-regrets. [Accessed 17 June 2020].

Maddock, Mike. "Making Tough Decisions Under Pressure." *Forbes*, https://www.forbes.com/sites/mikemaddock/2014/04/11/making-tough-decisions-under-pressure/. [Accessed 17 June 2020].

Morse, Gardiner. "Decisions and Desire." *Harvard Business Review*, no. January 2006, Jan. 2006. *hbr.org*, https://hbr.org/2006/01/decisions-and-desire.

"My 'What If' Choice." *Google Docs*, https://docs.google.com/document/d/1K1WrsUl-XxM8oonG9c3WSSMmWUe-A8O1odxxcAVwge7I/edit?usp=embed_facebook. [Accessed 17 June 2020].

"Narrowing Your Options Can Help You Make Better Decisions." *Exploring Your Mind*, 19 Jan. 2019, https://exploringyourmind.com/narrowing-options-better-decisions/. [Accessed 13 June 2020].

O'Doherty, John P., et al. "Learning, Reward, and Decision Making." *Annual Review of Psychology*, vol. 68, Jan. 2017, pp. 73–100. *PubMed Central*, doi:10.1146/annurev-psych-010416-044216.

O'Keeffe, G.S., and K. Clarke-Pearson. "The Impact of Social Media on Children, Adolescents and Families." *Pediatrics*, Vol. 127, No 4, 2011, pp 800-804, pediatrics.aappublications.org/content/pediatrics/127/4/800.full.pdf.10.1542/peds.2011-0054. [Accessed 9 June 2020].

Parenting Survival for All Ages. 2020. *5 Ways We Teach Kids To NOT Trust Their Gut Instinct!*. [online] Available at: <https://www.anxioustoddlers.com/gut-instinct/#.Xtwh9kVKhPY> [Accessed 6 June 2020].

Pigeonsuperstition.org. 2020. *About | Pigeon Superstition*. [online] Available at: <https://pigeonsuperstition.org/about/> [Accessed 6 June 2020].

Psychologistworld.com. 2020. *How Superstition Affects Us And What We Can Learn From Skinner's Pigeon Experiment.* [online] Available at: <https://www.psychologistworld.com/superstition> [Accessed 6 June 2020].

Psychology Today. 2020. *Gut Almighty.* [online] Available at: <https://www.psychologytoday.com/us/articles/200705/gut-almighty> [Accessed 6 June 2020].

Schwartz, B., 2020. *Is The Famous 'Paradox Of Choice' A Myth?.* [online] PBS NewsHour. Available at: <https://www.pbs.org/newshour/economy/is-the-famous-paradox-of-choic> [Accessed 8 June 2020].

Smarkets Help Centre. 2020. *How To Calculate Expected Value In Betting.* [online] Available at: <https://help.smarkets.com/hc/en-gb/articles/214554985-How-to-calculate-expected-value-in-betting> [Accessed 6 June 2020].

The Coin Flip: A Fundamentally Unfair Proposition? https://econ.ucsb.edu/~doug/240a/Coin%20Flip.htm. [Accessed 13 June 2020].

The Futures Wheel: Identifying Consequences of a Change. http://www.mindtools.com/pages/article/futures-wheel.htm. [Accessed 13 June 2020].

Verywell Mind. 2020. *Why Do You Always Make Bad Decisions?.* [online] Available at: <https://www.verywellmind.com/why-you-make-bad-decisions-2795489> [Accessed 8 June 2020].

Risk Impact/Probability Charts: Learning to Prioritize Risks. http://www.mindtools.com/pages/article/newPPM_78.htm. [Accessed 13 June 2020].

Samudre, Neal. "The Goal-Setting Recipe for Happiness: How to Craft Goals That Give You Joy." *Medium*, 22 Mar. 2019, https://medium.com/@nealsamudre/the-goal-setting-recipe-for-happiness-how-to-craft-goals-that-give-you-joy-abffc565c73a.

Susceptibility to Peer Influences (Psychosocial Development) – NJDC. https://njdc.info/susceptibility-to-peer-influences-psychosocial-development/. [Accessed 17 June 2020].

Tervooren, Tyler. "How To Make Great Decisions Under Stress." *Riskology*, 24 Apr. 2015, https://www.riskology.co/decisions-under-stress/.

"The Magical Number Seven, Plus or Minus Two." *Wikipedia*, 15 Apr. 2020. *Wikipedia*, https://en.wikipedia.org/w/index.php?title=The_Magical_Number_Seven,_Plus_or_Minus_Two&oldid=951074616.

Tschinkel, Arielle. "12 Unexpected Ways Anxiety Can Impact Your Life." *Insider*, https://www.insider.com/ways-anxiety-affects-your-life-2019-4. [Accessed 13 June 2020].

"We're Wired to Take the Path of Least Resistance." *Psychology Today*, https://www.psychologytoday.com/blog/the-gen-y-guide/201703/were-wired-take-the-path-least-resistance. [Accessed 18 June 2020].

Williams, Ray. 12 Dec. 2018. raywilliams.ca/neuroscience-can-help-us-make-better-decisions/. [Accessed 11 June 2020].

Yechiam, Eldad, and Itzhak Aharon. "Experience-Based Decisions and Brain Activity: Three New Gaps and Partial Answers." *Frontiers in Psychology*, vol. 2, Jan. 2012. *PubMed Central*, doi:10.3389/fpsyg.2011.00390.

www.ingramcontent.com/pod-product-compliance
Lightning Source LLC
Chambersburg PA
CBHW040107120526
44589CB00039B/2763